PERSONAL TSUNAMI

A JOURNEY OF FAITH AND FEELINGS

Jane Mill

Copyright © 2024 Jane Mill

All rights reserved.

ISBN: 9798335389167

Independently Published

Disclaimer
This book is my personal reflection.
I have recorded events as I have remembered them.
They are real events.
The people in the story are real.
I have expressed my personal emotions, thoughts and faith, as have those who have made their own contributions; but none of these are intended in any way to reflect the views and opinions of medical staff or anyone else involved.

About the Author
Prior to 2014, Jane Mill was a homemaker who also ran a successful part-time piano tutoring business. She and her husband Derek have 3 children and 5 grandchildren. They live in Norfolk and have been involved in their local Church for 30 years. This is her first book

This book is dedicated to
an unknown German gentleman.
And all donors everywhere.
Thank you.

ENDORSEMENTS

As a haematologist, I have too often been the 'bearer' of the news that instantaneously shatters someone's world. I am very aware of the weight of those conversations and see a phenomenal array of responses. I have seen people pushed to their physical and emotional limits and I usually get glimpses and some understanding of the impact on people's lives. However, I feel, that this is often a filtered or processed version that is presented to me. Even in their vulnerability, most people retain some degree of the great British 'stiff upper lip'. To read Jane's honest, raw account was incredibly eye-opening and humbling to me. She has approached the leukaemia, the transplants and all the ensuing complications and uncertainty with such grace, wisdom and utmost humility. She writes about how she doesn't like people describing her as an inspiration, but it is hard not to come to that conclusion! Her's is a faith and relationship with God that has been challenged, questioned, pushed to the limits, and ultimately remained steadfast.

Sarah Wharin, Consultant Haematologist, Leicester

There are heroes in these pages. Not the swash-buckling, hammer-throwing, sword-wielding sort. But the quiet, stand your ground sort. The pray till it's done sort. The I don't understand but I'm not giving in sort. This book tells of a life-story. It tells of love and friendship, family and fun. And it speaks of dealing with the prospect of death. Through it all, God is faithful. None of us can fully understand the processes of life and death. Nor will we ever fully appreciate the things we do not see - God's protection, often without being aware of it. The power of the Holy Spirit strengthening us from within when we most need it. None of us understands, but in these pages, we will learn a little more. My daughter Elspeth is married to Jane and Derek's son Rob. So, this is personal for me. As I read the words, there were times when the tears would come. Just the emotion of what I was reading, of what Jane and Derek had to go through. But also tears of joy. How God has been with them every step of the way. In remarkable ways. One day, every one of us will turn our face toward eternity. What will we say of the life we have lived? How will we reflect on the hours, days, months and years? In this book, we have a wonderful example of someone who stared at death and considered eternity with a pragmatic bravery. God-given bravery, no doubt. May every one of us be so bold. We can all be heroes.

Ralph Turner, Author, Leicestershire

This is a short and moving memoir of someone who faced a potentially fatal illness and is surviving the odds. It describes in unsentimental language that eventful journey. Many caring healthcare professionals routinely dealing with leukaemia may not appreciate fully, the nuances of patient experience of the people undergoing treatment. This memoir of a leukaemia survivor highlights in vivid descriptive detail, precisely that. The accuracy with which Jane describes her treatment is striking. Even for a trained professional eye, there is little error in her detailed descriptions of the treatments she underwent. What is most interesting in the memoir is how Jane never faults anyone, despite the ordeal she has gone through for prolonged periods of time; not a single bad word about anyone. It highlights not just the strength she draws from a clearly loving and close-knit family where everyone supports everyone else, but also an unwavering faith in God, even in the face of extreme adversity. Jane articulates the latter very well, but for the average reader left wondering if she, like most people, had at least some moments of doubt, there are reflections on that too in this thought-provoking book.

Dr Joe Joseph, Consultant Haematologist, Doncaster
Professor Regi Alexander, Consultant Psychiatrist, Norfolk

ACKNOWLEDGMENTS

What you are about to read here is not an individual project. I recognise that there were a crowd of supporters along the way, without whom this book would not exist.

I would like to thank the friends who have been kind enough to read my script at different stages, offering comments from a reader's perspective. Each one, Sadie Quinn, Joy Campbell, Ralph Turner, Regi Alexander and Joe Joseph have all in their different ways offered insights which have shaped the final book. Thank you all for your willing input and encouragement.

Members of my family, and several friends, have kindly made a written contribution regarding how my diagnosis affected them. For some of you, this was very difficult, and I want you to know how much I appreciate it.

Along the way I have received support from all my children and their spouses. Rob has always offered encouragement, Jenny has been instrumental as my sounding board on many occasions, and I would have fallen at every technical hurdle if it wasn't for George.

These past ten years have been difficult in different ways for each of us; some of which is shared in this book. But I want to personally thank my three 'children by marriage' – Elspeth, Sam, and Esther – all of whom have supported their families throughout. You are all wonderful.

Several people have been praying throughout this whole writing process. Thank you. You know who you are. My thanks go to Professor Regi Alexander, who has kindly been my editor and directed me throughout; and George Buschbeck, who was instrumental in preparing the script for publication. Dr Joe Joseph, whom I have never met, has been consistently helpful in pointing out times when I had expressed something medical in an unclear or incorrect manner. This list could, I think, go on and on, as there really are too many people to thank.

And I have not yet referred here to my husband Derek. That's because I don't know where to start. His support throughout my illness and the more recent book writing has taken an incredible amount of patience and kindness. When we made our wedding vows over 45 years ago, I don't think either of us really understood the enormity of "in sickness and in health, till death us do part." He has kept that vow many times over. And I want to thank him for it all.

Should my thanks to God have come first? Or here at the end? Maybe both. After all, He is the Alpha and Omega. May the words of my story bring glory to You. Thank you, Lord.

Jane Mill

CONTENTS

	Introduction	Pg 1
1	And so it begins: August 2014	Pg 5
2	All Change! August 2014-February 2015	Pg 19
3	Continued - August 2014-February 2015	Pg 31
4	The transplant: February 2015	Pg 45
5	Return to normal life? March 2015 onwards	Pg 65
6	And it's back: August 2017	Pg 91
7	What do we do now?	Pg 99
8	Second time round: May 2018	Pg 105
9	Another Assurance	Pg 115
10	What next? July 2018	Pg 121
11	Covid: March 2020 onwards	Pg 125
12	Here we go again: March 2022	Pg 135
13	What now? 2023	Pg 149
	Epilogue	Pg 167
	Postscript: May 2024	Pg 169
	Who's Who in the Story?	Pg 177

INTRODUCTION

This is the story of my last ten years.

It was never my intention to write any of this down.

I did not keep a journal throughout the time. However, early in 2023 I made the decision to address my memories in the form of a prayer journal, in an attempt to get my thoughts into order, as it were. I have kept that format, basically writing just as if I am speaking. While I cannot vouch for the exact timing of events, or their order, because I cannot remember them all, what I am able to remember are the feelings associated with different situations and conversations, and the challenge to my faith that they often provoked. Any conversation I have recounted is not intended to be a word for word account, but rather the gist of it, and the reaction it evoked in me as a result. These will be recorded in inverted commas. On the odd occasion I have used an exact quote, from a letter for example, it will be recognised by use of speech commas.

The James Paget University Hospital (also referred to simply as The Paget) is my local hospital, about ten minutes from my home. Addenbrookes Hospital is about two hours' drive from us. Both establishments feature heavily in the story.

Some friends and family have kindly been willing to offer insights into their personal experience regarding this story, as I am acutely aware that when any individual is ill, it affects not just the person concerned, but the people around. For many, this recollection has been a difficult process emotionally, so I am particularly grateful. Their experiences are recorded in grey boxes at the end of various chapters. It may also transpire that others' memories of timing and specifics sometimes differ from mine, but again, the focus is far more on how each step affected each of us or changed our outlook. Each contribution, including my story, was done independently, without reading the others'. The only exception to this is a further paragraph in chapter 3 from Jenny, in response to my recollection.

Certain songs are included which have been of particular help to me during this time. Title and author/performer have been included so they can be easily found on the internet and the readers might also find the lyrics encouraging.

I have endeavoured to be as honest as I can, both about the illness and what that involves, as well as the challenge it posed to my faith. Having been a Christian for over 40 years at the point of my diagnosis, I was about to have it put to the test, bigtime! Would it be enough when I encountered doubts, worries and fears way beyond my control? Although this is written from a Christian perspective, I hope that it can be helpful to people of different or no particular faith, in understanding some of the many complexities of a life changing illness.

Song:
'God is in this story' by Katy Nichole and Mike Weaver

The National Ocean Service describes a tsunami as
'a series of waves caused by earthquakes
or volcanic eruptions.'
The earthquake itself is unseen by the human eye, but
we do see the devastating effects
by the reaction of the water.

The Four Stages of a Tsunami

An earthquake begins on the ocean floor
The ocean floor cracks from the tremors
Tons of water rise high above sea level
A massive swell of water spreads out in all directions, affecting
everything in its path.

After the initial impact,
The extent of the damage becomes apparent
And the rebuilding begins.

It is not unusual to experience after-shocks.

CHAPTER 1
AND SO IT BEGINS: AUGUST 2014

The initial rumbling occurs on the Monday.
Although I am oblivious to this.
The wave hits the following day.
And I did not see it coming.

Tuesday, August 19th, 2014:
A date forever etched in my memory. The day when my normality ended. Life as I knew it was about to come to an abrupt halt. I found myself sitting in a small room at the James Paget University Hospital with my husband Derek in the chair next to me, being told that I had a life-threatening illness. How had it come to this? Was this really happening?

I was 57 years old, approaching my 58th birthday. I lived a busy life. I'd had a busy summer term as a part time self-employed piano teacher, and greatly involved in our local Church. In fact, I had just helped to head up an event at Church, which brought together and show-cased the many activities that were available in our village. Consequently, I was ready for a holiday. I was tired, but no more than I might have expected. Along with the above, I led a team who supported the "Young at Heart" (an over 50's group). We had fish and chip lunches, outings, quizzes, lunches at our house, trips to the theatre, boat trips, craft sessions.... all sorts. Oh, and a coffee morning every week of the year except the one between Christmas and New Year (we figured we needed one week off!)

It was a good life - busy but good. I also ran a weekly "Life Group"[1] during the school term. Derek, my husband, had retired in 2012 due to ill health. He had experienced a very serious bout of depression, culminating in early retirement

---

[1] This is a weekly small group meeting for people wishing to look at the Bible together and support each other in our faith

from his 30-year career as a teacher. He was beginning to recover by this point, and in fact had taken a small job at the local college doing some admin work and invigilation of exams to earn a little money. Money was tight, but we managed on the reduced pension, and my very small income. He had in fact just accepted the further offer of a 25-hour a week employment in the office at this same college. A nice, steady part-time job. Just mornings, from which he could walk away each day and not bring work home as he had always had to do. He was due to start that coming September.

Yes, life was falling back into place again, after a rough couple of years.

And yet, here I sat, listening to the words no-one wants to hear.

'We need to get it confirmed, but it looks like you have leukaemia'

Should I have seen this coming?

Some would say, yes indeed.

But hindsight, as they say, gives 20/20 vision.

And I did not have such vision whilst sitting in that small room in August 2014.

Derek and I had attended the New Wine Christian Conference with our Church that year as part of our summer holiday, camping on site alongside the other members of our Church, and it was whilst we were there, that I spotted 2 or 3 bruises on my legs, quite large but painless. Just a bit achy. I decided some support socks might be a good idea, so I visited a pharmacist for advice. Maybe I should have smelled a rat at his response to the bruising. But I didn't.

'I think that maybe you ought to see a doctor… There's actually a walk-in centre just over the road, if you'd like to go there?'

Why would I want to do that, I wondered? I declined his offer, promised I would go to my own doctor's when my holiday was over, and went back to the campsite to continue my holiday (without support socks!)

Sorry, Mr Pharmacist, but maybe you were on to something after all…

I thought little more of it and eventually we went home. We had lived in Belton, a village in Norfolk a few miles inland from Great Yarmouth, for the previous thirty-four years. This was where we had brought up our three children, who were now adults and had moved to new areas. Our summer holiday wasn't quite finished, as we had booked a week away with the whole family, (a first), down at a hotel in Devon which was completely to be paid for from our inheritance from my mum who had died in March, the previous year. She would have been thrilled that we had chosen to celebrate together at one of our favourite places.

Before that, there was a weekend at our daughter's to look forward to. Jenny and her husband Sam were by this time living in Derby. Approximately a four-hour car journey from the East Coast, we travelled there when we could, and would stay with them for a few days. Such a trip would almost always include a day in town for Jen and me. This particular Saturday trip, on the weekend sandwiched between our week of camping and the family holiday in Devon, started as any other. I did have an annoying tickly cough and a bit of a sore throat and reasoned that I was probably coming down with a cold, but certainly felt well enough for our day together. I don't remember any other detail about the day to be honest, other than I enjoyed it as always, but by about 3:00p.m., maybe 3:30p.m., we started thinking about heading back to Jenny's. And I remember quite suddenly thinking 'I really don't think I am able to do the walk back', so we called Derek for a lift. When we got back to the house, I remember taking myself off to bed for an hour or two before tea. This may be quite commonplace for me now but was not usual at that point in my life.

The evening passed happily as I recall, and Sunday morning came. We always like to attend Jen's Church when we visit there, and this Sunday was no exception. We had been due to leave Jenny's on the Monday, but by then, Derek and I had changed our plan. We thought it was probably best to make our way to Belton straight after Church, so I could contact the doctor first thing Monday morning as I was not feeling much better after my extra sleep. It was later that I first realised God had already been at work. I remembered the sermon that morning which was taken from Revelation 4. The text for the day had been simply "There IS a throne in Heaven and Someone is sitting on it." And it was a good sermon. This was to be a text that I would hold on to for reassurance for several ensuing weeks. In retrospect, of course, the visit to the chemist was also part of my preparation, I believe.

Back at home in Belton, Monday morning came, and I had my appointment at the doctors. The lady doctor I saw had recently joined the practice, and so was new to me. I said to her that I was mainly there because I was sending everyone in my family mad with this 'silly' cough… and we had a big family holiday the following week, please could she check me out? She looked in my throat, confirmed that I did indeed have an infection, and gave me a prescription for some antibiotics.

Simple.

'Oh, and by the way, during my holiday, I saw these bruises on my legs… and I spoke to the chemist… and he suggested I mentioned it to you… and I promised I would… so I am…'

The doctor looked at the bruises, handed me the prescription for antibiotics with the words, 'I think it might be a good idea to get a couple of blood tests done while we're at it… pop up to the hospital this afternoon.'[2]

I still did not twig anything unusual here. In fact, I thought that as she was new, she was being particularly thorough by covering all the bases.

Knowing what I know now, all sorts of alarm bells should have been ringing. But in those days, such worries were not even on my radar. Why would they be? But I dutifully went to the hospital and thought little more of it.

Blood tests done.

Normality restored.

---

[2] I later discovered that blood tests would feature heavily in my life! I have learned that blood can tell a lot about a person's health well before even the person knows themselves. Levels of platelets, potassium, magnesium, calcium and much more can be measured quite accurately. Blood tests can be used to assess general health, check if there is any sign of an infection, and to see how well certain organs, such as liver and kidneys are working.

Washing to be done for the holiday.

Plenty to prepare.

About 10:30 that evening I get a call from the hospital. How did I feel? Did I need to come into hospital? There would be a bed ready for me if I did!

Whyever would I want to go to the hospital? I had a sore throat for goodness' sake! I'm probably just getting a cold…

Out loud, (because I try to be polite!) I said, 'No thanks, quite honestly, I am fine' and he made me promise to go back to the doctor the next day to discuss the results of the blood tests. Again I promised, despite thinking that this was a bit strange… a bit of an overreaction… and got back to preparing for bed and a good night's sleep.

That Tuesday morning, the 19th, Derek had arranged an 11:00a.m. get-together with a friend who was trying his hand at music composition.

I am a little hazy about the order of events here, on this my last 'normal' morning. I may have rung the doctor as arranged, and heard the news that way or did she ring me first or did the hospital ring me directly? It doesn't matter. All I know is, an appointment had been made at the James Paget, could I go up there as soon as possible? Composition for Derek's friend, it seemed, needed to be postponed.

We were told to attend the Sandra Chapman Centre, and on arrival we were shown into the lounge and offered a cup of tea while we were waiting. I can't remember whether we accepted the offer – I probably did! This Centre has since become, at times, almost like a second home to me. There have been points in these latter years of my life when I have felt I belonged there more than anywhere else, including at home with Derek.

But on this day in 2014, I was totally oblivious to the fact that this was the cancer centre. I believe to this day, that God protected me so much from what was, quite a trauma. I have described it since as being "put in a bubble." A bubble of safety which I was in, in retrospect, for a good few weeks. It was almost like the numbness one can get after a sudden unexpected death. Some would call it simply shock. And maybe they have a point. But I believe even such shock itself is like a gift from God, whether we recognise it as such or not, because otherwise how could any of us possibly deal with huge loss all at once? And in my situation, I had no conscious sense of shock at all. I had had no bad news; I was simply being checked out… more thoroughly than I might have expected, it's true… but nothing to be too stressed about. Derek was not so oblivious, as I found out later.

So here we were in a small room, in the cancer centre of our local hospital, with a consultant haematologist and specialist nurse, (who was to be my "go to" person later) having this conversation about my health. I seem to remember others being in the room but am not certain. Derek may have different memories.

The questions I was being asked were along the lines of:

'Have you been excessively tired lately?'

'Not particularly; well, I was unusually tired this weekend just gone…'

'When did you first see the bruises?'

'A couple of weeks ago, towards the end of my holiday.'

'Your blood levels are very low. The most likely cause is something called Acute Myeloid Leukaemia. We'll run some tests to be sure, but it's looking that way…'

'Right…'

'So, we'd like you to stay in hospital today.'

'Right now?'

'Ideally.'

'Can I not even go home?'

'How far away do you live?'

'About ten minutes' drive'

'Well, you can pop home and collect a few things and come back as soon as you can. The sooner we start treatment the better. Before you go, we'd like you to have a test to check your bone marrow. But I'm pretty certain it will confirm what we think.'

'When will we know?'

'Within a day probably'

There was a long explanation of treatment, recovery time,

likely effects of treatment, most of which I sort of understood… well, I at least followed it at the time, but promptly forgot most of it soon afterwards.

'Is the treatment successful? Usually?'

'It's about 50/50 It will partly depend on whether you have a particular gene which may make it a bit trickier.'

'Ok…when will I know that?'

'We'll get that test result a little later, but we should know all we need to know by the weekend.' (This conversation was taking place on the Tuesday)

'Any questions?'

'Probably loads… but none I can think of at the moment.'

'Well, you get off home and collect a few things and we'll see you back here soon. There'll be a bed waiting.'

'Thankyou.'

And my life totally changed direction – it was as simple as that.

The whole process probably took about an hour and was beautifully handled. Straightforward and honest, but very kind, and somehow through it all, I felt safe. Safe with them. They seemed to really care about me.

I'd like to be able to say that the experiences of the recent weeks as described above, now started to make some sense to me; but to be honest they still didn't. Not until much later.

For now I was ok.

Safe with God.

Safe in my bubble.

So off we went, as per instructions and returned later to find my bed, which was indeed ready and waiting, as promised.

My husband, Derek:

We had been to New Wine, camping. Had a good time. Gone to Jen and Sam's afterwards. Jane had been out shopping in Derby with Jen but had come home earlier than expected as she felt tired and had a sore throat. Instead of coming home on Tuesday, we decided to come home early and try to see a doctor on Monday morning. This we did. I went with Jane and sat in the appointment. The doctor did her checks and then looked at some bruises Jane had. I can't remember if Jane pointed them out or the doctor did. As a result, we were sent for a blood test.

That evening, about 10 o'clock we were about to go to bed when the phone rang. Jane answered on the bedroom phone; I was on the landing. She told me it was the out of hours surgery. At that moment I heard in my head, quite clearly, "Leukaemia." I now believe that God spoke to me in that moment. Jane was told another appointment had been made to see the doctor.

Tuesday morning, we went to our surgery, saw the doctor and were sent immediately to the Paget. We met with a consultant and a specialist nurse. After a longish sort of explanation about blood etc. we were told Jane had leukaemia. I already knew and was so thankful for that word the night before; I was almost prepared. I went out into the car park and rang each of the children and simply told them what had happened. I was quite calm. We were in for a tough time.

My daughter Jenny:

19th August 2014

I knew it wasn't good when Dad wanted Sam to come home before he spoke to me on the phone. I started looking out my front door up the road (I can't remember where Sam was – but he was due back any minute [Edit from Sam – he was getting library books for our holiday – I had forgotten we were going on holiday] and pacing and wondering which direction he would come from. I didn't want to leave to meet him and miss him if he came a different way, and so as soon as I saw him come round the corner some long minutes later, I walked to meet him halfway up the road and told him something was wrong.

A few days earlier, when Mum and I had been shopping in Derby, she'd been very tired, and back at mine she'd also pointed out some bruises she had. I had thought at the time "If this was a film, it would be leukaemia" – in the same way that if a lady under 45 is waiting tables in a film and suddenly feels randomly woozy and faint, she's pregnant. Movie-cliché. But, in that long wait for Sam to come home, wondering what was going on, it didn't cross my mind once that that was what it actually was. I'd literally thought the word just days earlier – but that was not real life in my mind. I had forgotten all about it until Dad told us the news; and then the image of Mum showing me bruises a couple of days previously, sat exactly where I was sat right now hearing the news, came flashing to the front of my mind and I felt like I should have known.

I don't remember much except crying and crying on the phone. Then feeling bad because that was probably the last thing Dad needed, and I just had an overwhelming need to go home. I don't remember the exact timeline, but I know there were a couple of days between getting the news and when I was able to get home. I know I got the news on a Tuesday, and I think I was home on the Friday night and saw Mum for the first time on the Saturday but that bit is a bit foggy.

My youngest son, George:

Dad's phone call in August 2014 couldn't have come at a worse time. Esther and her mother were out shopping for wedding supplies, and I found myself alone at home, waiting on the floor for about an hour for someone to return. Looking back at my life, Mum's diagnosis marked a pivotal moment. At the time, Esther and I had a plan to get married in September, journey back to Germany (with a week on the south coast en route), and then fly to India, China and New Zealand for a six-month adventure. Both of us were living in Germany, with Esther finishing her studies, and no immediate plans to return to the UK.

Within a few days of Dad's phone call, we had flown back home. After one visit to the hospital, we found ourselves in the car park, making the tough decision to postpone our India trip. The aggressive nature of Mum's leukaemia left us uneasy about being so far from home. Following this initial decision, we began considering other options for the period after our wedding. Returning to Germany was a possibility, but we were both looking forward to the break that India had promised, having had a stressful season.

Esther (George's fiancée at the time, now his wife):

For most members in my family 19th August 2014 was the day everything changed. I think for me, it was a little before that. On 19th December 2013, our 3-year dating anniversary, George proposed to me. We spent the Christmas holidays sharing this wonderful news with friends and family and heading into 2014, our heads were spinning with exciting ideas for our future together as a married couple.

I am a planner. I always have been. I like to be prepared for things. So, when we got engaged in December, my initial thought process was something like this: well, it's going to take at least a year to plan the wedding. That would take us to December 2014 ... but I don't really want to get married in the cold, so we should probably get married the following spring. Perhaps in April or May? Yes, spring 2015 would be the time. It seemed logical, it seemed practical, it meant by the time we got married I would have pretty much finished my degree and could start looking for jobs.

But something about that plan didn't sit right with me. Yes, practically it made a lot of sense, but when I looked at where we were at in our relationship, the thought of waiting a year and a half before we would move in together and really start our life together (as I didn't want to do this until we got married), felt artificial. It was the second time in my life that I was faced with a major decision and while my head told me to do one thing, my heart told me to do another. Was it just intuition? Was it God? I battled with these thoughts for a good couple of months. I spoke to different people about it and got varying advice, but in the end, George and I decided that we would get married that same year in September.

Fast forward 6 months. It's the end of August and only one month until the wedding. We're about to travel back to England for a one-week holiday with George's family, when we get THE phone call. Life stands still for a bit. What are we going to do? A few days later we find ourselves in the hospital car park, having just been inside to see Mum. The next step is clear to both of us. We will move back to the UK for now. Whatever else we had planned could wait. We would have time… but we didn't know whether Mum would.

My friend, Jane P:

I can vividly remember where I was when I heard about Jane's diagnosis. We were visiting our son in Sheffield and I was working in his house when Derek rang. I sat at the top of the narrow stairs in his terraced house as Derek explained that she had leukaemia and would be starting treatment almost immediately. I sat there for a while after the call, trying to begin to process what this would mean for my closest friend: how it would be life-changing for her and her family, and how close it was to George & Esther's wedding. How serious was it? Would she survive? What would it all look like? I was determined to be there for her: she had been my constant companion through the darkest days of my life and I was going to be there in hers. Several times over the next few years I said to her: we walk this road together, wherever it leads.

Rosie, our Rector

'Utter shock at Jane's diagnosis after returning from New Wine'

Rosie's practical response was to begin a series of prayer cards for the Church.

PRAYING FOR JANE

Jane Mill has been diagnosed with Acute Myeloid Leukaemia (a cancer of blood forming cells in the bone marrow).

Please pray specifically for:

3or 4 ten-day cycles of chemotherapy (planned to start 26/27 August)

Sickness: that Jane will not be sick

Infection: Jane will be protected from any infections

Jane will know God's assurance & presence:
So do not fear, for I am with you;
do not be dismayed, for I am your God.
I will strengthen you and help you;
I will uphold you with my righteous right hand.
Isaiah 41:10

God's provision in all her need

Jane's family: Derek
Rob & Els and Jess, Jen & Sam and
George & Esther (wedding day 21.9.14)

Haven't I commanded you? Strength! Courage! Don't be timid; don't get discouraged. GOD, your God, is with you every step you take."
Joshua 1: 9

**Jane has asked that we all pray for our Church.
We are all part of the body of Christ, here at All Saints, Belton.**

1 Corinthians 12: 4-31
If one part suffers, every part suffers with it; if one part is honoured, every part rejoices with it. (v26)

So please pray for:

all aspects of church life

the times when we worship and pray together that we might have a fresh encounter with the living God

the groups that Jane belongs to/leads:
Young at Heart
Life Group at Paddock Close
Leadership Team

the gaps that will inevitably exist

for love and unity

for God to be glorified
and enemy activity not be successful

My friend, Shirley:

I'm struggling with words to write, as you know I'm not good with that sort of thing. All I know is I was devastated for you, Derek, your children and family when I heard of your leukaemia. It brings tears to my eyes when I think of it. I'm sorry I can't put my feelings into words. I'm here to support and help you in any way I can, then and now. Those words come straight from my heart.
   In God we trust.
   Your friend, Shirley xx

My friend, Pat:

After the phone call there was disbelief. I was emotional and scared that I was going to lose my dearest friend and scared for what you were going to go through.

CHAPTER 2
ALL CHANGE!
AUGUST 2014-FEBRUARY 2015

This chapter of my life in many ways brought about the biggest changes. And not only for me. How can I possibly put into words my response to the contributions from my friends and family? I can only try to imagine if I had had such news about one of them. If I had received a big shock, so had they. Different, yes. But equally significant. Derek finds it difficult to agree, but I have always maintained from the start of all of this, that it is worse for others than for me. Why do I say this? Because from day one, I had few decisions to make and everything in the hospital was geared to making me better. I voiced concern for my family to a nurse one day and her reply was straightforward.

'They will cope… you just concentrate on getting well, you'll need all your strength for that'.

Everything for me was now different. Unknown territory. But for my family and friends, their lives continued. On the face of it, to the casual onlooker, the daily situations they faced had not changed in the slightest. Yet inside there had been, to some degree or another, a significant shift. They were now carrying this new 'knowledge', which as you have seen, brought with it for some, a whole load of uncertainties and questions. And unlike me, they needed to process these whilst in the eyes of others it might be 'business as usual'.

It grieves me when I think of George and Esther changing their plans, and what must have been going through the heads of my other children?

Or my friends hurting?

I have always believed that no-one's illness is theirs alone; but reading these comments so many years on, it has become even more clear. There was little I could do about their worries; there was little they could do about my illness. In so many ways we all felt helpless. Yet the many comments made about simply 'being there' with me throughout, no matter how long it took, were priceless.

I had been an independent, healthy woman who kept house, was a mother of three children (now young adults) who did her own cooking, washing, shopping, cleaning, gardening and other related jobs around a home. Active in a team who held weekly meetings and arranged outings and events for a group of older folks, I also visited people who were housebound, and those in hospital. I taught a few piano pupils at my house, as well as teaching one morning a week at a local secondary school – having a small business which I had run for 30 years. I was also very involved in day-to-day Church life.

As from August 19th 2014, my life was lived in a hospital bed – alone in a small room – with a life-threatening illness – being woken daily at 6:00a.m. for blood tests – and regular observations[3] and receiving a cocktail of tablets and potions together with their interesting and varied side-effects. Hospital food prepared for me. (To be honest the first few days, when I had an appetite, this was quite a pleasure! No preparation. No thinking ahead. No washing up. And the food was good!)

The cherry on the proverbial cake was the chemotherapy. I had heard of it before of course, but it was just a word to me. This was administered through a drip[4] three times a day for ten consecutive days. After a few days of this, I'm not sure I could have been tempted to eat my very favourite meal from my favourite restaurant, if I had been offered it. The sickness and

---

[3] Observations include temperature, blood pressure and pulse and were taken 4 times a day and I was weighed regularly throughout my hospital stay.

[4] A drip is the term often used for an intravenous administering of some product. A blood or platelet transfusion works this way. There is for example, a bag of blood hung up high on a pole which then travels down a tube into your body. Often this is through an inserted needle into a vein. In situations like mine, however, there is often a more permanent device inserted, through which any product could pass. Mine was a Hickman line, inserted just lower than my shoulder, and became part of my body for this period – as if it was growing out of me. Painless, and very convenient, as without it I might have eventually resembled a colander – I would be so full of holes!

nausea were horrible. The least said about that the better. I suppose I should have been grateful, as I heard later that some patients who had relapsed at certain points were on a 24-hour regime of similar treatment in a desperate attempt to save their life. My "food" of choice – and even that was a struggle – was one of those 'meals in a drink'. A nurse told me much later, that one of those 'shakes' were the equivalent of a roast beef dinner – but I think the similarity stops there!

My room was an individual one, with my own bathroom, TV and a seat for a visitor. It was very comfortable. People have often felt very sorry – how lonely I must have been – but for the most part, I did not find it so. For one thing, as I outlined above, I was rarely alone long enough to get lonely as someone was always coming in to stick needles in me, taking blood or other specimen samples, or putting into my body whatever it was lacking at any given time. Lonely? Not so much. Sometimes as I got weaker, I craved sleep. But I have to say – and the nurses were always very apologetic about this – it did seem as though just as I was settled into a comfy sleep, there was 'something that needed to be done, sorry'.

The staff were, almost without exception, lovely. Very kind indeed. They would do anything for you, day or night, if they had the time. The nature of the ward, however, was such that an emergency could involve three or four nurses for an hour or more, and the more routine help was disrupted. I must say that I only heard about such difficult times in retrospect. Never did I feel I was too much trouble, even when they were rushed off their feet, nor for the most part did I feel rushed, except that I would have liked to go slower in the mornings. I was never a morning person and was less so now. But keeping me going – not allowing me to 'settle' into dependency – was of course, not unkind at all. It was part of maintaining dignity, and let's face it, I had lost most of that by that point.

Support

Another reason I wasn't lonely was because of my amazing family, friends and church community. So often people can feel they just don't know what to do or say, and can be tempted to back off and avoid contact at all. But as I would often say when this subject came up, I am still Jane. Still the same as I was, it's just that my body is sick. I cherished texts, cards, letters and messages. It helped me to feel that I still existed! I was out of 'normal life' but I still had feelings, was still interested in what was going on in the outside world, as it were. I was often not well enough to respond, but I was so glad to keep in touch in any way I could. Just knowing that people had remembered me - were praying for me, told me funny anecdotes, shared their news with me - was more special than they might ever realise.

Before embarking on this journey myself, I might have felt at a loss as to how to respond to a person in such a position as I now found myself. The following are a few of the many things people did for me which were priceless!

One of the first things Derek said to me was "We're in this together" and that meant such a lot. And from time to time over the years when things have got tough, he would remind me and I know he is still walking alongside all the time.

Over the whole nine months after diagnosis, I received a vast number of cards and over 60 letters, 41 of which were from one person, who often apologised for the quality of their "news", but I treasured each one.

I was sent inspirational verses and poems.

And things to make me smile,

Numerous gifts such as jelly babies or pastilles (many people wisely checking with Derek as to what my taste buds enjoyed at any given time!)

I received an e-card from a friend every day for months. How I looked forward to seeing those, again and again.

Activities to occupy me

A friend who is a keen photographer produced for me a beautiful book of her photos with the words of the song 'Blessed be Your Name' by Matt Redman superimposed. Beautiful to look at and very appropriate words.

Postcards from all over the country from our rector and another friend from Church. (These continued for a very long time, especially when I was missing an event that previously I would have been a part of).

Regular texts.

When I lost my hair the first time, I knew it was going to happen and it was the least of my concerns; but I must admit that when it actually started falling out, I realised I must have been subconsciously worried about what Derek's reaction would be. Because when he looked straight at me and said "You still look beautiful to me" it brought tears to my eyes. How very important these little affirming remarks are.

In addition, we were the grateful recipients of financial help. People sometimes don't like to talk money, but it is a fact that long term illness such as leukaemia – and there are plenty of others – come with many financial challenges. Loss of pay being but one. My "wardrobe" now consisted of many needed pairs of pyjamas, numerous nighties, slippers, underwear, personal products, and different weight dressing gowns. Gone were the days of one being worn, and one in the wash! Travel to and from the hospital and the subsequent parking fees for Derek. Trips to the hospital café for visitors who were there for some hours… there are many hidden costs.

Family support was incredible. Jenny, our daughter, had a job in administration – this is one of her many talents – and she was an incredible support. At that time, she had no children, and she arranged with her employer that she could for about 50% of the time, work from a distance, namely my hospital room. Nowadays, it is not so unusual, Covid is mainly to thank for that – but working from home in 2014 was not common. I asked her once, what would she have done, if they had refused her request? Her answer was at the time, and still is, amazing to me – "That", she said "wasn't an option", even if she had to resign. Some things were more important, she told me. Love in action. There were challenges to overcome however, all approached with a lot of prayer. Jen and Sam lived in Derby. Her dad and I lived on the eastern side of the country, and Jenny had no car. Nor could she drive. She was, however, determined to support me and her dad through this. By January 2015, she had undertaken an intensive driving course – passed her test – and bought a car and promptly drove back to Derby on her own. What would she have done if she hadn't passed? Apparently, that wasn't an option, either!

Passing the test was one thing, but could she and her husband afford a car? There was of course, their house deposit savings……….and yes they used that, eventually buying a house some four years later. To this day I am thankful for this sacrifice, just for us. Her attitude was simply that they would just do things in a different order. It may have involved more than this to them than I know, but I was I think, maybe protected from many things. And to be brutally frank, at the time I wouldn't have been in much of a position to argue.

We have an amazing family. Jen is just one – along with her husband, Sam, who was, and is, so understanding. Rob was married with a child and George was at the time, living in Germany. My husband, who was about to start his new job at the college, shared my care from day one. Between him and Jenny, or other visitors, I had someone with me most of the day. How uncomfortable it must have been tapping away on a laptop in a chair day after day. But what a comfort to me. I don't think they will ever realise the difference that made to me – even though I spent a lot of it asleep, or generally feeling groggy. Just knowing they were there was such a blessing.

A rather different birthday
One of the highlights during the initial couple of weeks was my 58th birthday, eleven days after admission. I was well into chemo and was feeling rough, but it was not the worst of days, health wise. Gifts were interesting, and very thoughtful. Nighties, jamas, dressing gown, slippers… If I remember rightly, Derek probably brought me in some fruity sweets (such as pastilles or jellies), about the only thing I could fancy at the time. Chemo did funny things to my taste buds – not dissimilar to pregnancy cravings, complete with nausea. And it could change from day to day. I must have been a nightmare to live with. Those around me needed incredible amounts of patience while facing such unpredictability. And how tiring it must have been for them. If I fancied coca-cola, for example (most unlike me) one would soon appear… I think the hospital shop did very well out of us during these times. And many a time, Derek would turn up with a selection of potentially fanciable goodies to see if any would 'hit the spot'.

Everything I ate or drank was recorded and I always did try to eat some proper food, but so often it appeared when I was just not hungry. And I craved strong tastes like fizzy drinks, pastilles or crisps. I did not take Derek's support for granted and many times I thanked God – and I hope, Derek too – that at least I had kept something down, and not given up eating altogether.

Some people eat in difficult situations. Comfort eating, I believe they call it. I have always been quite the opposite. Whenever I had been stressed at all in the past, I could stop eating altogether. This was an added challenge for me to overcome. But thankfully, when I explained this to my consultant and my nutritionist, I was allowed to have the "shake" drinks as my staple diet. Once the pressure of "you must eat, or you won't get well" was removed, I had far more chance of eating naturally again. I also had some information for them to put on their numerous charts!

On this first hospital birthday, our rector caused quite a stir, when she walked through the corridor to my room carrying twenty-one helium birthday and get well balloons, each with a message for me from my friends at Young at Heart. The balloons, of course are long since gone, but the messages are still tucked away in a box, for me to look at from time to time. Many from ladies and gentlemen who have since died. But I have the memory of more love in action.

My Church was amazing throughout this time. They collected for me and bought me my first iPad. Being quite old-fashioned on the technology front, I had no idea at the time what it even was, let alone how to use it! But it certainly was lovely to be able to have the occasional facetime chat. In fact, ten years later I still have it, although it is beginning to show signs of being poorly itself!

To cap it all, and finish off this amazing birthday, a cousin of mine called in to visit with her husband, along with a kindle (also a first)! Whatever were they doing here, I wondered? We were just passing, was the reply. This had to make me smile. I was in hospital on the east coast, and they live in Bristol! Love in action again. So what could have been a really sad time, turned into a beautiful day. Some things we do for people in difficult times seem very small (a packet of pastilles?), some are great gestures of kindness (a round trip from Bristol/ an iPad). It makes no difference to the recipient. I believe any act of kindness, no matter how seemingly insignificant, can make a real difference to a person's quality of life at any given point. So many people do not have such support. Also, we had no dependants. No elderly parents to care for. No inflexible employment. And of course, so many people do not know the love God has for them.

Jenny recalls her first visit back to Belton:

We arrived by train and Dad gave me a huge hug – he looked exhausted and just all wrong. I couldn't put my finger on the word to describe his expression. On one level, he was doing fine, and was holding it together well, but I knew that he wasn't doing quite as well as he seemed to be and I just couldn't put my finger on exactly what was giving me that impression. It was when we got back home and we carried the bags upstairs and I was heading back downstairs when I saw into Mum and Dad's bedroom. On Dad's side of the bed, the duvet was pulled back from having been slept in, and on Mum's side of the bed was all the clean laundry folded ready to be put away, from where she had left it before going into the hospital for an appointment, not expecting to be immediately admitted. I realised that Dad had just been sleeping next to the clean laundry for a few nights and I knew then that all of Dad's energy was going into keeping it together and looking after Mum, and that he would have absolutely nothing left over to put laundry away, cook, clean, and look after himself. That was when I first knew that I'd need to go home.

I spoke with Sam vaguely about the fact that I'd need to be spending more time at home before we had even seen Mum or heard anything about what was to follow. But everything that happened after that just kept confirming to me that I would need to be back at home. If I had been surprised by how adrift and ill Dad looked, I was equally surprised to see how well Mum looked. If anything, rather than putting my mind at rest, it added to the frustration of the whole thing; she looked totally out of place in a hospital bed, and other than the tears, she looked like she should just be at home. Upon speaking with her a bit, it became a bit more obvious that she was in shock but that mostly she was just worried about all of us. It was like we were having a perfectly normal conversation which suddenly hit me with little mini trains.

Mum was concerned about what it might mean for George's wedding. Train – I hadn't thought about that up until that point. Would Mum be at George's wedding?

She was excited about a second grandchild. Rob had called me to give me the news the same day we found out about Mum to give us some good news. Train – no one had talked about prognosis with me yet… would Mum ever meet grandchild number 2?

Another train in quick succession – even if she did, would Mum meet any of our kids if we had them?

Mum was worried about Dad – she thinks he's not doing as well as he comes across. Train – this is what is really on Mum's mind. Is Dad going to be okay?

We led worship that Sunday as a family, with the congregation facing the back of the church, which was a blessing. I was a total mess and couldn't do it at all. Everything looked so foggy and I cornered a doctor at my Mum's church, and peppered him with questions. He was very good, very clear, but left me in no doubt – the house had to be clean, Dad had to stay healthy and avoid coughs and colds and being run down, Mum had to stay germ-free and this treatment was going to take a long time. I can't remember exactly how the conversation ended, but I know it was the first time I said out loud "I think I'm going to have to move back home." I don't remember the reply exactly, but I know they didn't disagree.

For Jenny there were work implications:

When I went back to work, I booked a meeting with my boss immediately, to arrange for me to work from home. He arranged for me and him to meet with the head of HR that afternoon. They told me that it wasn't going to be possible for us to have an arrangement where I worked from home because then lots of people might want to work from home, but we might be able to arrange for me to have some more time off unpaid if I needed to go home a bit more. I told them immediately that I completely understood and that I tendered my resignation with immediate effect with my apologies for the lack of notice.

The head of HR was a lovely lady, and I remember looking right at her and saying "I'm really sorry – but she's my mum. I am going home to take care of her and my Dad. That's the right thing for me to do. I need to be with her as long as I can". She didn't say anything for a long time afterwards, but we spoke many months later and she told me that she had found it too hard to say anything. She herself had two young daughters (who she was always talking about). Unbeknownst to me, she was facing a very difficult prognosis herself as I was talking to her that day. She and my line manager spoke separately and agreed that I could work from home, as long as I was as discreet as possible about the arrangement because they were concerned about setting a precedent in the company. I owe them both a great debt.

I think about her and her daughters often and the look I saw in her eyes when I spoke about my mum and how I needed to be with her as long as I could. Sometimes people say "you'll never know how much it means to me… etc." but in her case, I know that she knew exactly how much it meant and that I'll be forever grateful.

Rosie:

Despite being in the midst of a devastating storm – Jane had real concern for the well-being of the church, and Derek and their family were strong in their trust of God. No one who was present will ever forget their singing of "Whatever comes" in our worship on the Sunday morning.

George:

The idea of returning to Norfolk was also on the table, but I anticipated challenges in finding enjoyable work, and I wasn't eager to return to village life, particularly as I felt like I'd only just left. We discussed other places in the UK where we could potentially live, ones that would allow us to reach home within a few hours. We had friends in Sheffield and Lincoln, but our main draw was to a new place where we hadn't been before. Ultimately, we connected with a couple leading a church in Leicester, and we asked if we could visit them on our drive from Germany back to Belton to see if it felt like a good fit for a season. During our honeymoon, we confirmed the decision that we'd land in Leicester and see what happened!

Jane P:

I had an update from Derek most days while Jane was on the cancer ward – but I just wanted to be there, to see for myself how she was, and to help if I possibly could. I never felt there was anything much I could do, so I don't think I helped her much, but it helped me to be with her, which always felt the wrong way round! I would drive straight to the hospital after school, change my clothes and then go to her room, taking my bag of marking with me. If she was awake, we'd chat – me sitting away from her in the corner of the room – Jane from her bed. We chatted about ordinary things – our families, work, things of interest to us both in the news or the village, just ordinary things as we would have done in our more normal times over a coffee at the garden centre or café. We talked about going out for coffee again many times over her years of treatment: it was a goal for us both, I think. Jane did say to me that she appreciated our chats as we didn't focus on her illness and it brought some normality to her situation. There were times when we prayed together, or I prayed for her, but I prayed more on my own – often several times a day as she crossed my thoughts at home or at work – simple prayers for God to heal her and for her to know his presence. I was at times in awe of how calm she seemed, how she seemed to accept her situation with grace and to hold onto God in it all.

If she was sleeping, then I would just sit and get on with my marking. I was happy just to be there. Occasionally, she slept all the time I was there, unaware that I'd been, but that was fine with me. I remember how once, when she was struggling emotionally, we'd held hands, and I was moved to tears, because I missed that physical contact. We had been through some really difficult times before and had always been able to give each other a hug, or hold hands in empathy, and it felt strange not to be able to offer this physical support to each other in these times.

CHAPTER 3:
CONTINUED
AUGUST 2014 - FEBRUARY 2015

George's Wedding

Almost a month to the day from my original diagnosis, was my youngest son's wedding day. He was to marry a young lady from Germany, and they were at the time both living in that country and studying at university there. Their plan was to get married – take 6 months off to travel – then back to Germany to finish their studies, at which point they would look for jobs.

Another of our children changing their plans. The wedding took place. I could of course, not attend in person, as I was not well enough. However, I was very kindly allowed home just for the day, where I took up residence on the settee and watched the service on my TV, a live link having been set up from the Church. How kind they all were to do this. As the congregation left the ceremony, many walked past the camera with a wave and a smile. That was special.

Prior to diagnosis, I had bought my dress for the day, along with a wide brimmed hat… my other children were married and, as the groom's mother, it could be the last occasion I was ever likely to wear such flamboyant headwear! So, on the day itself, I donned my dress and hat – that was as far as my outfit had been purchased – and had my photo taken with two friends who kindly missed the wedding on my behalf. One of them in everyday clothes, one in Bermuda shorts! My Hickman line was showing slightly at the dress neckline, and my hat putting into shadow the remains of an eye haemorrhage, which had spread previously down one side of my face, making me look rather like a character out of a Sci-fi programme! I also had no hair. It was not the most conventional look for a wedding photo, but how special it was to me! In addition to this, George and his bride came to see me, along with Jane P, and were photographed with me as well. So, I can now proudly say I was in a handful of my son's wedding photos! Everyone did all they could to involve me in the occasion, and it is another kindness I could never repay.

By mid-afternoon, my temperature spiked to 39.9ºC and I began to experience the rigors[5]. The first time I had experienced these had been while I was an in-patient – that is, as a patient on a ward. This was fortunate for me, as it was initially quite scary because I seemingly had no control of my body, and I was desperately trying to stop myself from biting my tongue as it felt as if every part of me was shaking. As with many other symptoms such as these, as time went on, I became more adept at spotting them earlier so they could be addressed. So thankfully, I knew what was happening to me at this point, but this was my son's wedding day and somehow it felt different. Another friend who had popped by to check on me refused my pleas for 'just another hour' and promptly bundled me into car/wheelchair and took me back to my hospital bed. More love in action. I remember very little of that trip or the next 2 or 3 days, other than they were rough. But as I said to the nurses later, I wouldn't have missed it for the world!

Beginning to adapt
This first 6-month on and off stay in hospital was local, fortunately for us only about a ten-minute drive. At that time, I was told that the James Paget typically had 2 or 3 patients a year with my type of leukaemia, and this year was no exception. There are however many patients in very similar circumstances; and opportunities arose sometimes to share our experiences. At the time, I knew very little about leukaemia – only that it is a blood related cancer. I did not know there were many types. Over the years, I have become much more informed.

There were also many opportunities over these months, to

---

[5] A sudden rise in temperature can be an indication of an infection and is a particular cause for concern in someone with little or no immunity. The rigors are episodes in which your temperature rises – often quite quickly – whilst you have severe shivering accompanied by a feeling of coldness 'the chills'. The fever can be quite high and the shivering may be quite dramatic.

chat with different patients in the shared lounge and we sometimes talked about our own individual experiences. There was always a mixture of people at varying stages of many different types of illnesses, and I soon became aware of the seriousness of different situations, including my own. I had, rather naively, been under the impression that I would be back teaching by the coming Easter of 2015 – just missing 2 terms and picking up where I left off with any pupils who had not found alternative tutors. I had expected to be teaching at least another fifteen years. After all, my own college piano tutor was still going strong, and was well into her seventies! So, I watched others' progress with interest. I would take encouragement from any 'ahead of me' in their journey, whilst also being aware sadly, of those whose health was declining. On any given appointment date, I would wonder if certain people were there to chat to. There was one lady who I met there, and we had a great deal in common. At one point we were even in adjacent rooms during an in-patient stay, and whoever was the better at the time, would pop 'next door' to have a quick chat. I think it is fair to say we both enjoyed those few minutes each day, and talked of getting together when we were well. In my head she was what I might term a 'not-yet' friend; but our chatting was natural and easy. Then suddenly, she wasn't around for a while. When I asked after her, I was told the news of her death. She was not the only one, but the one loss that saddens me most. It was difficult.

In hindsight, I could see God had been preparing me, protecting me every step of the way, and I was not let down during these months either. It was a time of amazing closeness to my Father God. I slept badly, and every time I was awake overnight, I would pray individually for our Church congregation back home and sent regular short notes when I was up to it, to keep in touch with people. I found out how true it was, that when all the "distractions" of life – good or bad – family, hobbies, work, timewasting, even ministry are taken away, what are we left with? Who are we left with? Our Father God, with whom I talked at every stage and whose comfort and strength I had relied on all through.

I wondered at the time, how in practicality, I could possibly maintain such closeness in a more "normal" situation, with its necessary day–to–day commitments. I believe it was a rather special period of my life, spiritually. A time when I particularly needed that closeness. I was totally dependent on God and others. Of course, we are always totally dependent on God, even when we do paid work, or raise families, but it seems to me to be so much harder to maintain in the busyness of life. Is it that we need to work harder at the relationship? Or is that just me? It certainly changed in quality when I felt better, and since God never changes, I can only acknowledge I moved away somehow. Sad.

Song:
'Whatever Comes' by Brian Doerksen & Steve Mitchinson

Realisations

As a result of my first bone marrow test[6], it had transpired that I did indeed have the extra faulty gene, which reduced my chances of survival percentage wise. As I struggled with this, a wise friend of mine (one in the medical profession), advised me by saying 'It's just numbers. Basically, for a survivor, its 100%'. That helped. Because of course, it is true.

I had a stream of local visitors, sometimes more than the nurses thought was good for me, but how lovely it was of everyone. One friend from another Church brought me a prayer shawl. Apparently, a group of them got together regularly and prayed as they were knitting. A prayer in every stitch, I was told. How precious. My rector very early on, had given me a holding cross. I have never really been someone who uses aids to prayer in this way, but this proved vital to me. I held it in my hand as I settled down for each long night, and simply feeling it there at any point I was particularly 'down' was a great comfort. I know it has no 'magic powers' but just

---

[6] A bone marrow test is a way of extracting a sample of marrow from the patient's pelvic bone by a rather large needle. The sample can then help determine the presence of a blood disorder such as leukaemia. The procedure is done under local anaesthetic.

the feel of it in my hand was a physical reminder of the love of God for me shown ultimately through the death of Christ. This period also began a real change in me as to how I talked about my faith, and what God was doing. I remember being incredibly calm and matter of fact about it. It was so real. So natural. This could have been due to me still being in a state of shock. I still tend to see it as being my God-bubble of protection. Whatever the cause, (and whichever it was, I believe God was behind it), my faith was truly tested, and God proved true to His word.

One friend came to visit, who found it difficult to accept even the possibility of me not coming through. *Please don't talk about that.* I was not negative, quite the opposite. As gently as I could I simply explained that this was indeed the situation. Getting well was not a given. I might die. Seeing they were visibly upset, I got out of bed, no doubt attached to various drips, and then was told they should be comforting me, not the other way round! But it works both ways, doesn't it? As we aim to bless others, we ourselves are blessed. This assurance of God's presence, and my secure future whatever transpired, was so real and so powerful, that it was something I could share. The 'ill' person does not always need to be the recipient of blessing. There is no hierarchy in God's economy.

Yes, I seriously had to face up to the possibility of an earlier than expected death. In fact, I came very close one day.

A very different appointment

Jane P had come to an outpatient appointment with me. At each appointment during this period, three times per week, my blood was monitored, and it was decided what, if anything, I needed on any given day; red cells, magnesium, potassium… My main need at that time was platelets, the means by which blood is able to clot. Bleeding, along with getting an infection, are the two main fears with leukaemia patients. I had had plenty of platelet transfusions, a simple, painless procedure that was administered by a drip, and would take about 20-30 minutes from start to finish. As an aside, the satisfactory standard platelet count for an adult is between 160 and 370. Almost always I asked for my number, mainly out of curiosity.

I may not have had a clue about what these numbers meant, but it gave me an idea of which direction I was going in at any given time. My record, believe it or not, was basically the equivalent of *one platelet*... I decided to call him Peter!

This particular day began as any other, but soon after the drip had been started, I said to my friend Jane, that something wasn't right. I didn't feel right. She called the nurse over, who immediately fetched a wheelchair. I remember being wheeled out of the room we were in, into the corridor – then nothing. My next waking memory was of being surrounded by doctors and nurses, along with my friend, and Derek and Jenny who had been called in. And I had itchy feet. When I looked, they had huge hives on them. Apparently, I had been covered in them, and I had been pumped with antihistamine to counteract the anaphylactic shock I had apparently experienced. As I was coming round, I can remember simply saying "Father, father", whether that was audible, I have no idea. When I awoke, apart from my "itchy boots" which Jane was looking after with calamine lotion, I felt fine. I was kept in overnight as a precaution and had a stream of nurses come in to see me at one point or another, joking about me being a troublemaker, to which I would reply that I liked to keep them on their toes! One came in, very apologetic, hoping I hadn't got sore ribs, as she had been performing CPR and hadn't 'held back'. One who had been in the room at the time, asked my permission to use the experience as part of her on-going training. So, I may even be in a case study somewhere!

The first Christmas
Christmas 2014 was very emotional for me. I have 3 adult children, the eldest of whom, Rob, had a wife and young daughter. Rob, who lived near Cambridge, had been in touch regularly all throughout, and had brought his wife and 4-year-old daughter to visit, the latter thoroughly enjoying riding up and down on the hospital bed. My daughter-in-law was also pregnant with their second child, due in the March. That was very much on my mind.

Would I ever meet and hold him or her?
Would they have found a donor match for me?

Would I hold out till then?

Would a transplant even be successful?

One of the most special things I remember about Rob's visits was that he always took me to one side and prayed with me before he left. I wonder if he ever knew how much that meant?

As a family, we tend to have celebrated Christmas in our own homes, and have whenever possible, met up in Belton for a few days over the New Year period. Due to all our family commitments through marriage, this is a real treat for us, as it is the one occasion a year when we try to get together all under one roof, even if the four families only overlap for the one day. This Christmas Rob's family chose to come to stay with us, and the others joined them later. It was so lovely. Incredibly special, of course, as I think perhaps it was on each of our minds that it may be our last Christmas/New Year together.

What will 2015 bring?

My transplant was pencilled in for Jan/Feb 2015. This is known as a stem cell transplant and in my situation involved the removal of my cells, followed by a transplant of someone else's into my body. These bone-marrow stem cells are instrumental in producing blood, which in turn, determines a person's state of health. For example, a dearth of red blood cells could explain the cause of someone's lack of energy; too many white cells can be a sign of the body having an infection; some elements such as lymphocytes and neutrophils are infection-fighters, so too few of them can result in difficulty when trying to overcome illness. The transplant basically meant that my diseased cells would be removed and replaced with healthy ones. My body would then need to decide whether to accept or reject them. All 'foreign bodies' (think of a thorn, or a germ) are treated as an enemy, and all the blood defences are alerted into action as part of the healing process. It is as if our body knows there is a threat to it and aims to annihilate the problem. Initially the new blood cells might be considered a threat - 'These don't belong here' - and my body could try to get rid of them. During this period, I would have no defence against any illness or infection.

So I was, by this point, painfully aware that reaching the transplant was by no means a 'given'. I took nothing for granted and learned to be thankful for every positive thing, no matter how small. Maybe I had eaten a little something; I had received a letter; I sat up a bit longer; I was saving money on shampoo…(!)…; and if the shower-drain at home was clogged, my hair wasn't the culprit! Regarding hair, during this period I lost it two or three times, although it did attempt to grow back in the long recovery periods between treatments. By the time I eventually emerged back into the outside world, my totally straight hair had become very tight curls. My family and I joked that I looked like a poodle – and long-standing friends were known to pass me by in the street! It was quite nice, really, having curly hair, as I'd had to pay a crazy amount of money to get my hair curled previously, and it had never lasted long! Another thing to be thankful for later, I would say, although when people commented on my new look, I did suggest that the route I chose to get curly hair was not really to be recommended. 'Pay the money' was always my advice!

Humour aside, these six months had been fraught with infections, which was why I had been so poorly and in and out of hospital. After each round of chemotherapy, my bloods would be weakened. So, then we had to wait for the blood levels to recover in order that they could administer the next course. This would often take weeks and was quite a scary and vulnerable time. This treatment was to continue until such times as all was in place for the next step - the transplant, with all the new risks attached to that.

On a visit from my rector, I said I needed to talk to her about the possibility of dying and being ready. As a result, at the age of 58, a day or two before the end of January 2015, I hastily put together my funeral wishes, put them in a sealed pink envelope, and gave it to her to hold on to. Then I awaited the call to go to the hospital where the transplant would take place. A two-hour journey from Belton to Addenbrookes Hospital, Cambridge.

Rosie:

George & Esther's Wedding Day – and Jane unable to be there. I remember we did our best to provide a live link via iPad. Tracey getting dressed up – smart top & hat (but with her shorts on as it was a lovely warm day). I also remember feeling a righteous anger – how could Jane miss such an important day in her son's life?

Pat:

George's wedding. I was upset that you couldn't attend your son's wedding and celebrate with your family. I couldn't think of you being on your own and was glad you could watch it, although the day was too much for you.

Derek:

One of the things that was really difficult for me was when I got a few days at home and people were ringing to ask how Jane was. This was even more difficult at church where it seemed as if everyone was asking the same thing and I kept repeating the same information again and again, usually pretty ghastly! Eventually I asked the rector to put a note in the notice sheet asking people not to ask me and I would update either in the notice sheet or by speaking to the church directly. This just about solved the problem although one or two people still asked but I was better equipped to speak to them. Sometimes Jenny would "head them off at the pass" and answer on my behalf.

Jenny:

September 2014 – May 2015
It's strange – when I was first asked to write for this book

about the impact that Mum's cancer had on me and my family, it is this period that immediately came to mind vividly. But it's been by far the hardest to write about. Not emotionally, but just practically. Everything was in a weird time-jelly – I have no clue what order things happened in. There were so many details every day with intense ups and downs, but I look now, and it is just a blur. The closest I can think to describe it is to remember the first COVID lock-down. Unusual emotions, sudden new change of routine and rules and habits. A time that can't be compared with any other time because it feels self-descriptive – its own ecosystem. When I remember these months, I have a feeling in my chest as if I'm suddenly back in it, and all the sounds, smells, habits, thoughts, worries all come as one big mishmash of stuff that just IS that time.

I remember concluding I needed to drive. I booked an intensive 2–3-week course. I was getting the train to learn to drive, working for 30 minutes on the train, having a 3-hour driving lesson, working for 30 minutes on the train back. Going to the hospital and working next to Mum whenever she slept or was feeling unwell and not wanting to talk. Going home and doing the laundry, trying to cook a meal, doing some more work and going to Tesco very late at night. I felt totally wired all the time. My sleep was all over the shop, but everything was lists and "work 4:20p.m. – 5:05p.m. – add 45mins to the work hours this week" and "which medication makes Mum very sick?" and "who's on the rota to see Mum today?", "has Mum and Dad's council tax gone out?" and "how many hours behind at work am I?" We didn't have the money for the car, and I don't remember how we did it. I genuinely don't know if we added money onto our bank loan, or emptied our savings or were given money or anything. I have tried to remember and looked back through our financial records, but I can't work out where the money came from and have no recollection of dealing with the finances/insurance or anything at all. I just remember buying the car.

One day when neither Dad nor I was there, we got a call

to say Mum had had an anaphylactic shock and that she had had to be resuscitated and was now stable but not awake yet. We both dropped everything and went up to the hospital, praying on the way. I remember being glad I wasn't a driver yet because I had no idea how I would have driven feeling that scared. It was the most surreal thing. Mum had technically died, and we'd just been at the house doing our work. I felt a huge guilt that I hadn't been there. It was, if I remember correctly, the first day I had chosen not to go in because Mum had said she was having a better day and I was miles behind with work and Dad knew straight away that that's what I was feeling and told me in no uncertain terms, as gently as he could, to stop it. I really struggled for a while afterwards with that and it made doing the visiting rota much harder for a while- one of the many times where my emotions and my logic didn't function well together during this time. That night, I remember just breaking down on Dad and saying, "What if I never get to tell Mum that I'm pregnant and I have to do it all without her?" It was one of the only times in those months that we cried together, and it was a real relief to me, because I hadn't really seen Dad crying and I hadn't really cried in front of him much since coming home. It really helped me, in a strange way, as it felt like we were speaking the same language in that moment rather than both being in our own different "coping" modes. For me – having rotas, lists, spreadsheets made me feel like I could control the uncontrollable, and it was always hard when that illusion was broken, and I realised that I couldn't do anything meaningful to change what was happening to Mum and Dad.

Jane P:

Occasionally, I took Jane to the unit for treatment as an outpatient. I was able to stay with her and chat while she was on a drip. On this day, we were sitting in a large waiting room, with many other people, both patients and visitors, sitting chatting or reading around us. The nurse connected her to the drip, turned it on and left while the treatment took place. Jane & I were chatting when she said that she was feeling a bit strange. Very soon, she stopped talking and became less responsive, just sitting in her chair, in the middle of the room. No-one else seemed to notice. I left the room to get help from the nurses' station and they came quickly. By the time I returned (which was a matter of seconds) Jane was becoming unconscious. She was whisked out of the room, and it became clear this was a life-threatening situation. The crash team was called as Jane was taken into a side room and I was asked to wait outside. I had no idea what was going on. They asked me to call Derek, which I was already doing, and ask him to come. I was worried she wouldn't be alive by the time he got there. I remember feeling anxious but not emotional – I was in shock but also in practical mode. What could I do to help? Who did I need to contact? Was there anything at all I could do to be useful? I stood outside her room, feeling helpless and anxious as people came and went. In what seemed quite a short time, the nurses said I could go in and sit with her. This was my first indication that she was going to be OK. Remarkably, Jane seemed quite coherent and calm, able to carry on a conversation. I think she apologised for giving me a fright. We sat and I believe she had a cup of tea – the solution to everything! By the time Derek got there, she seemed fine. I left them together. As so often, this incident affected me more afterwards than at the time. I wondered what might have happened had I not been there: no-one had noticed she was unwell. I am grateful I was there as I'm not sure she would have survived if not, which is a scary thing to reflect on and is something I've found a little hard to carry.

Jenny reacts:

Having read some of the other excerpts now, it occurs to me that this event could have been so different if Jane P had not been there to raise the alarm. Although I struggled much, much, less with Jane as a visitor, as I think of her as family anyway, reading these other perspectives back has made me realise how hard it must have been being one of the people who was not there throughout, as Mum's anaphylaxis was my biggest experience of not being there when I wanted to be and it was really awful. It was hard watching Mum go through the whole experience, but it must have been so much harder to be far away. Strangely, on this particular day, I had absolutely no memory of Jane being the person who called, or being there at the hospital - reading that was like hearing about it for the first time. It is all a total blank. All I remember was the guilt of it not being me, and a long drive there - I don't even remember arriving or seeing Mum afterwards. Now, I just feel so grateful to God that Jane was there when Mum needed her.

Esther (now George's wife):

We get married on 20th September 2014 and 10 days later we move to Leicester; a new city where we don't really know anybody but where we're welcomed into a church that immediately loves us and cares for us and supports us through one of the most difficult times in our lives so far. We spend the first 3 months as a married couple living with a family of five, applying for jobs and praying for a miracle! It's a tough time for us and I can only draw close to God and trust in his faithfulness. We had been living in Leicester for about 5 months when God spoke to me about our future. It happened in a way it had never happened before – so poignant, direct – and for the third time in my life I make a decision that from the outside seemed completely irrational yet in God's big picture somehow made sense. We decide to stay on in Leicester and I quit my degree.

Meanwhile, a bone marrow donor for Mum is found and she has a successful transplant! She lives to see her second grandchild being born that March and we are beyond grateful. Mum's diagnosis changed the trajectory of my life (and our marriage) completely. It was tough. And as time went on, I was often battling with guilt when I found myself feeling frustrated about the things I had given up in order to stay, knowing there was a much greater loss for my mother-in-law, whose entire life had been turned upside down and would never be the same again.

How would I cope if I had been present with a good friend who basically became unconscious in front of me, was whisked away into a small room by the medical staff, and I was told to call their relatives? Or if my dream of going travelling for 6 months with my new husband was called into question because of an illness in his family? Or if my mum couldn't be at my wedding, and the whole situation had the potential to overshadow my special day or mean that she might not be around when I had children? Or if the money I had painstakingly saved for a house deposit was suddenly taken to pay for driving lessons, and the whole situation would pull me away from my new husband for months? I can only surmise. And be eternally grateful that there was the willingness to put aside plans and dreams for me. I can never repay that.

CHAPTER 4:
THE TRANSPLANT: FEBRUARY 2015

A transplant had it seems, been part of the plan from within the first few days of diagnosis.

I have been seen and treated by a team of consultants and have been amazed at how they all seem to work 'as one' in that I don't have to go into each appointment needing to give a lengthy account of my medical history. The very first time I had a meeting about a potential transplant, I was quite poorly. I was an in-patient at my local hospital undergoing chemotherapy and I remember very little about the meeting at all, to be honest. I must have looked a sorry sight, and, as someone unable to engage with any sensible conversation, I'm amazed they even thought of me as a good risk for a transplant! But I am extremely grateful they did

Moving to the unfamiliar
So, this was now really happening. I remember thinking this is the sort of thing that happens to other people, not me. But here I was, looking ahead to this medical procedure to quash the disease living within my body. What would it entail? What would it mean for me and my family? Staying in Addenbrookes, a hospital a two-hour drive from Belton, would bring its own challenges.

Would I get visitors from home? I had had lots of them at the local hospital.

What would Derek do about work?

If Derek was not the one staying with me when we were back at home, he had worked out a great system of popping in to see me two or three times a day. He had the timing down to a fine art. Each visit was within the permitted half-hour free parking. He took great delight in the fact that he could visit regularly and not pay! I don't like to think of how much we would have paid in parking otherwise. Only later did we find out that there was a subsidy for visitors of long-term patients

– but to be honest, I don't think I would have counted as such. Although I spent most of the six months as an in-patient, my stays were interspersed with the odd few days when I managed to avoid a temperature, at which point I was able to go home. He had also recently started his new job and was loving it. And, because he had needed to take early retirement from his teaching career, we really needed the extra income. But how often would we be able to see each other now?

Until this point, we had become familiar with the appointment system at the James Paget Hospital. I was getting to know the staff on the ward, and they knew me. It had become for me a comfortable place. I felt safe there. I knew what to expect and what was expected of me.

How different would it be in Addenbrookes?

There was talk of isolation. Visitors would be limited due to risk of infection.

What exactly did that mean? It was certainly too far to commute!

What would the transplant entail?

This transplant, like any invasive medical treatment brought with it many implications.

The disclaimer I needed to sign was all-encompassing:

Possibility of organ failure (heart, lungs, kidneys, liver – all quite important, I've heard!), Secondary cancers,

Reaction to chemotherapy – 'Chemotherapy is itself toxic of course, and will do your body harm while we are tackling the leukaemia…'

Infection – 'you will be kept pretty isolated as you won't be able to fight infection very well. We'll treat any infections with antibiotics where we can',

GvHD: Graft versus host disease[7]

In extreme cases, death.

---

[7] The graft is the stem cells or bone marrow from the donor. The host is the transplant patient. GvHD happens when particular types of white blood cells from the donor attack the patient's own body cells. This can result in illness – acute or chronic and can cause a series of further problems. (The Bible tells us we are fearfully and wonderfully made, and our millions of body cells are programmed to protect us from outside threats to our health, so maybe this reaction is not really surprising).

And this, I needed to sign! It most definitely felt like I had to just 'go for it'. It was to be all or nothing. What choice did I have? I seem to remember saying something to the effect of 'Well, I don't really have much choice do I?' to which the reply was in effect, 'No, not if you want to stand a chance of beating the leukaemia'

I signed the form.

How did we cope?

Was it my 'strong faith', as some describe it, which helped me? I'm not sure that I actively did anything strong. Sometimes I simply saw it as passing the buck. My thinking went more like this: 'There's absolutely nothing I can do about this.... You say you love me... so please do *something...*' That sounds more like weakness to me! Imagine a lifeguard swimming out to rescue a man in difficulty in the sea – he says, 'I've got you, just let me carry you to shore'. Is it better to fight or relax? The drowning man is still in trouble, probably still scared, but if he can relax and let the rescuer get on with it, a lot of burden must be lifted. He is no longer alone. But he wouldn't benefit from trying to show how strong he was, but rather to accept he is not. It was like that with me. Did it make it easier? Yes, in many ways, certainly emotionally, if not physically. I had enough to deal with already, without the added pressure of trying to be strong. The simple fact was that I was helpless, and I let go of the responsibility of what was going to happen. As with many things in life, when God is in the life picture, things started falling into place. Questions answered. Worries relieved. Why do I doubt it each time? Why do I go through the whole worry scenario before remembering He has never let me down yet...?

Accommodation and work

There had been a patient who was previously treated at this hospital, and had later sadly died, aged only 24. She had begun a fundraising initiative which her mother continued after her death by means of a trust fund set up in her memory[8]. The money raised was specifically designated to fund on site "free-at-point-of-need" accommodation for relatives of leukaemia patients. Those who could afford to, would be able to give a contribution in retrospect.

Derek, like so many before and after him, was the recipient of this gift and was offered a small flat. Like a hotel room really, with desk, wi-fi, TV, and ensuite bathroom. There was also a fully equipped, modern kitchen shared by occupants of the adjacent flats. The whole place was amazing. Clean and well-cared for, it meant that Derek could keep on top of his laundry – and mine – and cook rather than face the expense of eating out. What a blessing was given to us and so many before and since because of a family tragedy. Some might say that has nothing to do with God, or faith, it was simply the kindness of another human. I can't argue with that, of course, other than to say that as I get older, and read into God's Word, it seems God is and always has been the instigator of the good in the world.

For everything God created is good, and nothing is to be rejected if it is received with thanksgiving
1 Timothy 4:4 (NIV)

Dear friends let us love one another, for love comes from God
1 John 4:7 (NIV)

Every good and perfect gift is from above, coming down from the Father of the heavenly lights who does not change like shifting shadows
James 1:17 (NIV)

And as Einstein famously said:
"There are only two ways to live your life. One is as though nothing is a miracle. The other is as though everything is a miracle."

---

[8] Karen Morris Memorial Trust – wonderful charity!

To us at this time, it was a miracle. And how thankful we were. So Derek settled in and worked there around visiting hours as allowed by his boss. Another kindness. He was permitted to work more flexibly, so didn't have to keep to college hours, although he was able to work from my room when necessary. Because the days were long, and I was often not much company, Derek came out of that period approximately 42 hours in credit! So, in this way, accommodation was sorted. Income could continue and financial strain was minimised. His work did not suffer greatly.

On the health front, nothing nasty transpired for me in the way of serious reaction, organ failure, or the like. I fought the infections and tablet side-effects as well as anyone could, I think. God was providing for us in so many ways, but as we know, He never promised us an easy ride. As Jesus told his disciples not long before his own death:

'I have told you these things so that in Me you may have peace. In this world you will have trouble. But take heart, I have overcome the world'

John 16:33 (NIV)

Physically, it was difficult. Emotionally and spiritually, I felt very carried during this time, and as I have previously said, almost protected.

Church was a wonderful support.
Even as I write this, my heart goes out to those who don't have the care and support I enjoyed. What I can say is that I owe a heartfelt gratitude to my Church family and friends, and hope that in some way, I might in the future be able to offer similar support to others. My rector, Rosie, prepared an up-to-date prayer card regularly providing people in the Church with current prayer topics which included both thanksgiving and petition. There were times when I could almost physically feel the power of the prayer. It was a very vulnerable time. Things were happening to my body which were scary, sometimes painful, and often quite undignified to say the least. People in

similar positions can understandably want to keep things private. This I totally understand and respect, and I was certainly selective about which ailments to share and which not. For me though, when I think of Church as a family, and that we are encouraged to be specific in our prayer, how could I avoid being more forthcoming?

We can pray, "God bless…*name*…in hospital" or
"Please make…*name*…better"

And both prayers would be answered very generally, I'm sure.

But what about the following prayers?
"*Name*… has an infection in their throat" or
"*Name*… has mouth blisters" or
"*Name*… needs a donor who is compatible, and the doctors haven't found one yet"

These prayers require specific answers.

Throat infection gone.

Mouth blisters gone.

Donor located.

Such answers to prayer are great faith builders!

And even aside from missed prayer opportunities, it is very difficult to support anyone practically if we don't know a little something of their needs. It is a difficult call for all concerned, and we choose our own road in this area.

My stay as an in-patient, during which the transplant took place, turned out to be five weeks and a couple of days. A bonus considering the six weeks I was prepared for. During this time, my daughter – now driving – shared the accommodation back-to-back with her dad, allowing her dad to be at home for a few days at a time. I'm not sure if I knew at the time and had forgotten, or whether it was one of many things I was shielded from, but Jenny did not pass her driving test first time. This I am certain would have caused her anguish, not to mention more expense, but I do remember her passing the test on her birthday, in time for helping during my stay in Cambridge! Sometimes we may wonder 'what skills could I bring to a situation like this? I'm not comfortable around sick people. I can't even cook a casserole…' But what about organisational skills? Not worth anything?

My daughter has a real flair in this area, and it was exceedingly useful. She could help her dad with organising the flat, food and laundry. Not that he couldn't do it himself, but it freed him to think about me, his work, and created the time to process some of his own feelings, rather than simply being busy, busy, busy. Give Jen a problem which can be helped by a spreadsheet, and she is in her element! She kept a record of my medication (which changed regularly, and often), what date they were prescribed, what it was for, and if there were any side effects. Given that I had about 40 a day, there was no way I could remember them all, so when I had a nasty reaction to a couple of them, she was able to find a record of all the details! We can all use our gifts in some way or another to support others, if the occasion arises.

Let's be frank with each other
Maybe one thing all of us can do, is to listen very carefully. Being heard, and our feelings being accepted for what they are, is of great importance. It certainly was for me. Being told that I 'shouldn't feel that way' was not helpful. Close friends often helped me with putting my thinking more in line with God's word, but even then, it only really took root at times when I was able to hear it. I wonder if that makes sense to you, the reader. I suppose there aren't many of us who like advice thrust upon us when we are struggling, no matter how good/well-meaning the advice given is! I was fortunate enough to have friends and family around me who would let me have my rant for a while; and it was interesting that, in the relief that came afterwards, in the weariness of it all, I was in a much better place to listen to a gentle word spoken to move me on. Have you ever tried to reason with a screaming child, mid-tantrum? It was a bit like that! At some points in my illness, I felt as if all my resources were taken up in surviving the urgent, present symptoms. Logical thinking was not always high on my agenda.

It can be like that with practical help too. No doubt we've heard the story about the person who, on seeing a blind man standing by the side of a busy road, spots an opportunity to do a good deed. Consequently, they take his arm to guide him safely to the other side. Despite the blind man's protestations, he was nevertheless accompanied to the other side of the road and the 'good Samaritan' went on their way, still unaware that the blind man was not ready to, nor did he even want to cross the road! 10 out of 10 for good intentions, but not so good on the listening front. A joke, yes, but a reminder that help is not actually help if it is not helpful!

I know, even as I write, that I have done the same and most probably will again. In fact, I have, very recently. Simply because I am in the unenviable position of being on both sides of this sort of situation, I am maybe more able to consider the challenges from both viewpoints. When I gave this some thought, I concluded that it seems to be, again, down primarily to listening. Asking questions such as:

"Is there anything I can do to help?" is a very kind offer, but it would require me to think of something and I was likely to respond with a 'no, I'm alright, thanks'.

On the other hand, 'Would it help if I…….?' is a question which just needs a 'yes please' or 'no thank you'. Far more likely to get a 'yes please' in response!

I am aware that this is easier for those with a close relationship, but even for the more infrequent visitor, the question "Would you like to talk or would you like quiet?" can be very refreshing. These are just my thoughts, and of course, everyone responds differently. The bottom line for me was just knowing that someone cared enough to offer, and then subsequently listen to my answer.

Looking ahead

Prior to my transplant stay, unbeknown to me, Jen had contacted different people and Churches she had links with, and many gave a small gift, one for each day I was there! They came in the shape of an inspirational verse, a picture to colour in, a jigsaw to make up, a poem to read, something their children had made in their Church group, a bible verse to encourage. Something I could do on an "as and when" basis. Being remembered in this way meant so much to me. It was another connection with the outside world. Another small reminder, that behind the drips, commodes and energy drinks,

I was actually still me.

A nurse had, prior to the day of transplant, explained to me that previous patients had described the actual procedure itself as rather an anti-climax, as in fact it was simply another drip! So, when the time arrived, the drip was put up, and the only difference between that, and previous transfusions I had received, was that it was a bright orangey sort of colour and a nurse sat at the door for the 45 minutes or so that it took place, watching me intently for any sign of immediate reaction. If I remember rightly, I sat and ate my tea talking to Derek whilst it was happening!

It was from this point on, that my immunity dropped to its very lowest. Basically, all the bone marrow cells that made up 'Jane' were removed. Everything that my body had in place to fight any infection was gone. And we waited in anticipation for the new donated healthy marrow to start taking up residence in me, to do the job that mine couldn't do, because it was sick. The waiting for this to take place was estimated to be about 3 weeks.

I do like a pattern

This continued to be a difficult time, but gradually throughout the following weeks I slipped into a sort of daily pattern:

6:00a.m: woken for bloods and 'obs' (observations such as blood pressure, temperature, pulse, usually, 3 or 4 times a day), get weighed. (this was almost daily, and was due to the implications of not eating, as much as anything)

7:30a.m: cup of tea

Between 8:00 and 10:00a.m.: breakfast, wash, dress for the day, and if well enough, sit out in the chair. Usually Jen/Derek would be there about 10:00a.m. This was my "fun" time. If well enough, this might mean a bit of colouring or reading if not, simply company in the room.

12:00-2:00p.m: Dinner or whatever I was having followed by rest time, as prescribed by doctors. No visitors; although ironically, the tests and doctors' and nurses' visits did not always stop!

Afternoon was like the morning when I was able. Occasionally I would have a game of cards with Jenny or

Derek – a real highlight. Sometimes I would have a different visitor, one of the boys, or a friend.

5:30p.m.: Another break for teatime, not a great joy for me, as I was still 'grazing' throughout the day and night when I could. I would watch a couple of quizzes on the TV and this helped to pass the time. Jen or Derek would come along in the evening too.

Between 9:00 and 10:00p.m.: Preparing for the long night. Having a programme to watch was rather a blessing, and I became quite reliant on something to watch to keep me occupied before the long night began.

When I see it written down, it all looks quite organised and pleasant. And in a way, on a 'good' day the regularity was a comfort, it gave a good structure to the day, and any person in the room was company and often resulted in a short conversation. But when I think back as to why the days felt so difficult sometimes, I realise that all these key events were interspersed with regular bathroom needs, being sick, trying to get down and keep down tablets, trying to drink enough, eat something, regular 'obs', (blood pressure temperature, pulse, and probably other things I was not even aware of), cleaners' visits, and regularly being asked by medical staff for information to update their charts! There were constant bell noises in the background, giving me a sense of how the day was going for the staff. And everything I tried to do took so long! There was no energy to move. Everything was hard work.

Overnight there was not a lot of sleeping, but I had pre-recorded music on my mp3 player that Derek had prepared for me. Very helpful it was too, as it included a fair amount of worship music which was lovely to listen to even in the middle of the night, and this would often be accompanied with, or followed by, a time of prayer. There was a lot of praying. Nights were long, but with the major difference that there were fewer interruptions – just the 2-hourly check to see all was well, or if I called for assistance.

The Staff
Such a lot is said in the media, and by many people, about the

problems with the NHS. And I know there are problems-significant problems. But no-one within my hearing range can get away with being negative about the people involved. The doctors and nurses involved in my care have shown themselves to be among the most selfless, patient, servers of people that I have met, even in the extreme pressure under which they work with being short-staffed, short of equipment and time, to name just some of the challenges they face daily. But the people themselves are amazing. My care throughout has been second to none.

The five weeks were difficult, but with the support of all my family and friends it was far better than it might have been. My "boys" were very involved with their jobs and families and kept in touch as often as they could and a visit from them was a real highlight as you might imagine. I have often thought, that in some ways it must have been particularly difficult for them in a different way from their dad and sister. Being away from the situation, they maybe had less of an idea of what was a 'good' or 'not so good' day for me. I think, looking back considering this period, what mattered to me was knowing that they and my friends remembered me. It was not a question of 'out of sight out of mind', or 'can't do anything while she is in hospital'. How important it was that I felt involved in normal day to day situations, even if I was not actively involved, or couldn't even respond. After several weeks in hospital or being housebound, it is extremely easy to forget what life on the outside is like. And as time went on, questions arose in my mind; how would I fit in, if and when I got better, as all the gaps I had left would be filled?

As we left to go home, early March 2015, I looked back to see the wooden plaque hanging above the main reception desk which says something along the lines of 'Whatever it is, It will pass' and indeed this part had. As Derek wheeled me to the car for the drive home, he asked me how I was feeling at that moment. I had 2 main responses as I recall: I was relieved to be going home and I never want to go through that again.

Pat:

Your first transplant was on my birthday – scary. There were all the times we couldn't see you, give you a hug – or you hug me – when we needed one!

Derek:

Jane was diagnosed on 19th August 2014. I started my new job as an administrator on 1st September. Strangely I only thought about how I felt when Jane had virtually finished the book. Finding out how I felt was quite difficult, and I discovered quite a few things. Having known in advance, I believe through a word from God, made it easier to deal with. I told Jane we were in this together, and I meant it although I had no idea what I meant! Most of the time I was on autopilot, simply doing whatever was needed at the time. Jane wanted a crumpet; I toasted a crumpet. If we didn't have any I went and got them, plus spares. Her tastes changed at the drop of a hat, cherryade out, limeade in. Cheesy puffs yummy, cheesy puffs yuck! Go to get some bacon rashers. We played endless games of rummy, and Jane was struggling, so for a little while I was in the lead. That changed when she had better days.

At home I visited The Paget at 8:00a.m. for 25 minutes, at the end of my five-hour morning at work for 25 minutes and then I parked on the road and walked over to spend the evening playing cards and watching TV, until about 8:00p.m. or sometimes later depending how Jane was feeling. As time went on, I got more and more tired, but somehow adrenaline kicked in and I just kept going. (25 minute visits also meant I avoided parking fees).

At Addenbrookes, I had a flat to live in free of charge through a charity. Life was totally unreal. I went to the ward at about 8:00 in the morning then went back to the flat to work for an hour then back to visit. I worked for the two hours I had to vacate the ward at lunchtime and anytime I could during the rest of the day when Jane slept. I also worked when I got back 'home' until the early hours, usually until about 2:00 or 3:00a.m. I was up at seven to start the day again. I made up a lot of time at weekends and when we came back to Belton after five weeks, I was 42 hours in credit. I wrote most of them off as I was so grateful to the college and my line manager for allowing me to work from where Jane was.

A side effect of living like this was my weight shot up! Cooking for myself was mostly fast foods; burgers, fish and chips, bags of crisps and nuts, and a few cans of beer more nights than was good for me. I still battle with my weight today. Just one of those things.

Jenny:

The flat was another one of those little ecosystems that just sits totally separately as its own standalone thing. It had a strange sense of home for a few weeks and the walk between the flat and the ward every day felt like a weird "normal." Every now and then, I'd have this sudden sense of "none of this is normal!" It's not normal to have a spreadsheet for whether it's me or Dad sleeping in a flat and to change bedding on handover day. It's not normal to meet at exactly at a certain point to hand over a parking ticket so that the other can leave on the other parking ticket. Hug, exchange a few words about the biggest thing happening in our lives, and then handover and be on the way home. It's not normal to shop at a Marks and Spencers in a hospital for your main meal or, if energy permits, down the road in a local Sainsburys that becomes weirdly familiar. But I think all those things helped to keep everything else going. The little rhythms we had, the random texts about how many potatoes we've left behind, helped to make a not normal situation feel a bit more normal.

The hardest thing to write about emotionally has been seeing Mum poorly. There were some really difficult days.

A text from Dad to me, or me to Dad, or to the family might have said "not a good day today" but we all knew to read between the lines. The not-good days were bad days. We did have some lovely days where we'd be laughing and joking and talking about all sorts of things and playing Bohnanza and I have some precious (and funny!) memories from those times. It wasn't all terrible. But there were days where I looked at Mum, and she was skinny and bald, and she would lie down with her eyes closed if she was feeling nauseous and her mouth just looked so sad. Other days, she would be sat up and struggling to lift the straw of her water cup to her mouth and she just looked like she was dying. And I would be sitting looking at her, and just praying that the next good day would come. There was one particular (unusual) occasion where Dad and I overlapped at the hospital for about an hour – I can't remember why. Mum looked very ill and was lying down with her eyes closed. Dad was just sat next to her holding her hand – I think he was praying. I felt like I shouldn't have been there, because I was interrupting something so intimate just being in the room. But this sudden fear filled me that it was nearly the end – and that I was seeing the last moments of dedication in their marriage. I took a photo of them that I still can't look at without crying. Whenever I think of "in sickness and in health" – this is what love looks like to me.

Jane P:

Some of the hardest times for me were when Jane was in the hospital so far from home and I couldn't see her. There were periods when she wasn't well enough to text or call and I was reliant on messages from Derek to know how she was doing. I didn't ever want to add to his load so tried not to hassle him by asking, and he was very good at keeping me informed. I am so grateful he and Jane made the decision to let me visit her when it was safe to do so – it helped me so much. The day when she had her first transplant was tough. I knew there was a possibility it could go drastically wrong and I was on edge, waiting for news, knowing it may not be good. I vividly remember going to see her afterwards, driving the two hours down to the hospital, feeling apprehensive as to what I would find, not knowing quite how to act – until I saw her and things were as they always had been.

Jenny:

Mum had a list of people who were on the visiting rota. Some were "any-time" people, some were "if I feel sick and tired and just want to sit still" people, some were "If I feel miserable and need cheering up" people and some were "only if I'm already having a good day" people. Trying to make sure the right people were there at the right time was one of the hardest jobs. Me and Dad both had work we needed to do, we both needed a break where we weren't at hospital and we both wanted Mum to have company and the right people with her. To be perfectly honest, I didn't want anybody else to see her. I just wanted it to be me and Dad and Mum (and my brothers when they were home). Every second not with Mum was harder, and I had to pray a lot about feeling resentful that other people were getting quality time with her and were hearing her speak and how she was thinking and feeling. I knew there were thoughts and feelings that she would share with different people at different times, but I really wanted to be there all the time. I knew it was selfish – but I didn't want anyone else to have any special time with her other than our family. It sounds awful – especially as I know how much she meant to other people – and I'm very grateful (now) for their support and love. But sometimes at the time, I just felt like screaming "she's not yours, though!" When Mum came out of hospital, I was told to "be a bulldog" about who came near Mum and when. I was to have no qualms about refusing entry to anyone who I was not sure was the picture of health and might introduce germs or might not be the best person for Mum to see on that day. That was an easier job!

Doubts

Did I never have any doubts? To that question, I would start with what may feel to some like a 'politician's answer'. Because it very much depends on what is actually meant by the question.

Did I ever doubt God exists?

No.

Did I ever doubt whether He is who He says He is in the Bible – all-powerful, all-knowing, loving, compassionate, a shepherd, a father…?

No.

Did I ever question "Why me?"

No. (Why *not* me?)

Did I never have any struggles with my faith at all?

Oh yes. Many. I had struggles more than I could count. I certainly questioned His methods. I wondered whether I was doing something wrong somehow.

What more can I say?

I didn't question whether God really existed. But I would certainly challenge Him quite vehemently as to what was He doing. I identify more readily these days with the writers of the book of Psalms, a book of songs found in the middle of the Bible. They are exceedingly honest about their struggles with God and His ways. Take for example Psalm 73, which I interpret as a psalm of two halves. It begins as the psalmist looks at the horrors of the world around him and almost harangues God with sixteen verses of incessant ranting. The following is taken from Psalm 73 in "The Message", a version of the Bible which is one person's interpretation, putting into his own words the feeling he imagines lie behind the psalmists' words (italics are mine) :

" [1-5] No doubt about it! God is good—
  good to good people, good to the good-hearted.
But I nearly missed it,

missed seeing his goodness.
I was looking the other way,
   looking up to the people
At the top,
   envying the wicked who have it made,
Who have nothing to worry about,
   not a care in the whole wide world.
   6-10 Pretentious with arrogance,
   they wear the latest fashions in violence,
Pampered and overfed,
   decked out in silk bows of silliness.
They jeer, using words to kill;
   they bully their way with words.
They're full of hot air,
   loudmouths disturbing the peace.
People actually listen to them—can you believe it?
   Like thirsty puppies, they lap up their words.
   11-14 *What's going on here? Is God out to lunch?*
   Nobody's tending the store.
The wicked get by with everything;
   they have it made, piling up riches.
I've been stupid to play by the rules;
   what has it gotten me?
A long run of bad luck, that's what –
   a slap in the face every time I walk out the door.
   15-20 If I'd have given in and talked like this,
   I would have betrayed your dear children.
Still, when I tried to figure it out,
   all I got was a splitting headache…"

As I read this, I can almost feel the frustration… he had tried to live well… he had tried to honour God… and look where it's got him… what's going on? I could empathise to a certain degree in my situation as I queried Gods seeming lack of action at times.

Then the pivotal verse 17.

"Until I entered the sanctuary of God.

Then I saw the whole picture…"

I imagine him, in his rant, almost holding his breath, going red in the face, and getting more and more worked up – until verse 17 when he starts to calm down, and breathe again. And he starts to see his situation in light of the bigger picture.

Have you ever experienced the tantrum of a young child? When the child doesn't like what their parent has told them to do/not do? They don't understand it, don't like it, so they yell, accuse, stamp, beg or plead. The parent stands firm, knowing that they are acting in the best interests of the child, allowing them to express their frustration until they break down in sobs in their parent's arms when their anger is spent, and they eventually start to accept that on this occasion, their parent is not going to back down. Their sobs subside. They start to breathe more normally again. Quietening down. They are safe.

Is the child questioning whether the parent is there? I doubt it!

Do they understand any more about their parent's actions or words? Maybe, maybe not, depending on their age and ability.

But the bottom line is this:

The parent is the parent and the child is the child. That is the relationship within which they function, whether they understand it or not. Whether they like it or not. Even when they kick against it. But within a healthy relationship, it is a safe place to be.

Did I have struggles?

Yes. Many.

Did I question what God was doing?

Yes.

Did I always like and agree with Him and His methods?

No.

Did I feel safe with Him?

Yes, when I got to the point where I accepted – yet again – that He is God and I am not. And I would figuratively speaking, breathe out, let Him put His arms around me and I relaxed.

Did I question whether He loved me?

Not really. I was just wanting to understand more.

From my point of view, if I'm honest, I often felt like grumbling to myself, that that wasn't a very loving thing to do, or even, 'if I were in Your position, I'd have done it differently....'.

Laughable!

How limited my view is compared to God's.

How little I see other than what affects me.

Not unlike that of the young child in the earlier example.

What a minuscule view of the 'big picture' I have.

God is God and I am not.

I have often reflected that I was indeed fortunate to have known God as my heavenly father for 40 years or so prior to my leukaemia diagnosis. Hence, I started out from a position of safety and a certain amount of trust in the relationship, although my faith was surely tested throughout this period. That is not to say that it is necessary for one to already know God to receive His comfort, only that it was helpful. Imagine the situation I described earlier, the same in every aspect, but rather substitute a good foster/adoptive parent. Because the parent/child relationship was not already established, it could feasibly take a little longer for the child to trust the loving authority of the person whose arms they were in, simply because they were yet not sure of their love. But the outcome could be the same.

Hence the 'politician's answer' to the initial question did I have doubts?

Did I doubt He existed? No.

Did I doubt He loved me? No.

Did I question how He went about things? Certainly.

I am encouraged to some degree by an event described in the gospel of Mark in the New Testament, in which there was a man with a sick son who came to Jesus for help.

"Speaking to Jesus he wonders "If you can do anything, take pity on us and help us."

[23] "'If you can'?" said Jesus. "Everything is possible for one who believes."

[24] Immediately the boy's father exclaimed, "I do believe; help me overcome my unbelief!""

Mark 9: 22b-24 (NIV)

These last ten years have been for me something of a rollercoaster ride. And it continues to be so, as there are many ups and downs even now. Like everyone else, I do not know what the future holds, and therein lies a problem for me. Because I am a planner, I think it would help to know, so I could plan. But there is a reason God does not tell us our future. Simply because it is not in our best interests to know. He does know, though, so He can do the planning. That's my logic speaking.

Emotionally I struggle with that because I want to maintain control. In my calmer, more lucid moments however, I must acknowledge that out of the two of us, probably - just probably - God is better at this planning than me! If I had been made aware at the age of twenty, that thirty-seven years later I would get leukaemia, what would that have achieved for me?

Would I have still wanted to have children? I almost certainly would have worried about details (that I knew nothing of) and tried to manipulate circumstances (over which I had no control)! I couldn't have a changed a thing for the better. And almost certainly, any such knowledge of my future, and its inevitable effects, would have spoiled my present at any given time. I need to remember that even now. Ultimately, I have to trust the One who knows.

Do I have struggles?

Yes.

CHAPTER 5:
RETURN TO NORMAL LIFE?
MARCH 2015 ONWARDS

My recovery felt slow.
When I was in the first hospital after diagnosis, I had said to my named nurse that I hoped to be back to my piano teaching by Easter, assuming that my treatment would last no longer than two school terms. Her response was that my initial "signing-off" period would be one year, and then we could take it from there. I can see now that I had been rather naively optimistic – but I knew so little about the nature of the disease at that time and I was innocent enough to think of it in terms of:

>I get ill
>I go to the hospital for treatment
>Yes, it might take a while, a couple of terms even
>I get better
>Life resumes

I also remember saying to a nurse just before I left Addenbrookes after the transplant – in a very chipper manner – "Well, onwards and upwards!" In retrospect, another naïve statement. I remember well her reaction. She sat on the edge of the bed (a most unusual action, and a sure sign to me that I should 'listen carefully') and said something to the effect of 'You mustn't think like that'. She explained that my recovery would be slow and I still had to be very careful about infections. I was to expect stays in hospital during this period – this was the norm. And one particular thing I remember quite vividly – probably because it was the last thing I would want to hear – 'And there will be days when you feel far worse than you have in here.' I was stunned by this. This is surely not how recovery should be?

The recovery graph in my mind looked like this:

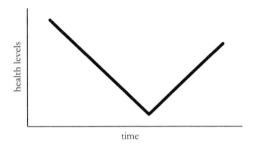

In reality, it proved to be more like this:

The nurse's caution was one of the best pieces of information I was given, and I reminded myself of it many times in the following weeks and months. Because she was right. And I am the sort of person who would rather hear the truth than have it hidden.

Eating had become no easier for me except that I had more opportunity for 'picking at' things I fancied. I have never been one to fuss about food – I would eat / try almost anything – but I was certainly fussy now. Because in these early days I was still neutropenic, (i.e. my immune system was very poor), there were lots of dos and don'ts (not dissimilar to when a woman is pregnant).

I was to avoid reheated food, particularly meat.

Only accept food that has been 'prepared to the letter of the law' sort of thing.

No carveries (you never can be sure how long the food has been sitting out)

No unwrapped sweets or biscuits (you don't know who has touched them and there was the possibility of a cross-infection) - if there's a bowl of peanuts on a table, for example, which have had different fingers in, don't take any.

This also posed a potential barrier to receiving help. It is one thing to offer to bring a meal over to help us out, but there were so many limitations to consider. I was very fortunate that I had friends who took the trouble to find out what was 'safe' for me and cook fresh, as I was advised not to have any reheated meals. Caring for or supporting a person with a long-term condition requires long-term commitment. It is sacrificial in many ways, especially when it cannot fit around your schedule. (Someone might in this situation, for example, usually make their casserole/lasagne/pie the day before or get one out of the freezer). I was so very grateful when someone cooked for us, and of course it meant that Derek had a night off. Friends would drive me to the hospital and pick me up at some indeterminate time when Derek was unavailable. Having someone with you when you attend appointments is helpful; if only to have available another 'set of ears', as the patient themselves is not always capable of asking pertinent questions, or even remembering the answers afterwards. I was very grateful that Derek was, in the main, able to do this for me, but others are not so fortunate.

Anti-bac was now my friend and it accompanied me everywhere. Derek and I were expected to mask up in all hospital settings, partly for our sake, but also for that of other patients. Anyone who had even a sniff of a cold couldn't come in to see me. Hugs were out. Visitors were asked to antibac their hands at our front door as a regular thing, way before it became the thing to do during Covid. This is something we can all keep in mind, I suppose. Whenever we visit someone with any long-term underlying illness, to do everything we can to protect them in this way. When a body is constantly fighting an illness, whatever it is, there is less resistance to other more common illnesses such as colds, sore throats and sickness. Young children can pose particular challenges, as they are picking up all sorts of bugs and germs at their nurseries and schools as they themselves build up their own immunity. It was a hard thing not being able to see my granddaughter very often (aged 4) but thankfully these days there are many and varied opportunities through technology to continue. Not to forget the old-fashioned 'snail-mail'! Children love to have the postman bring a card addressed to them!

I did, however, take one calculated risk within days of leaving the hospital, when, on a journey home from one of my follow-up appointments, we called by to see our new-born granddaughter (2 days old, just out of hospital herself!) and we have a very special photograph of her in my arms. It was still in my mind at that point, that it might be my only cuddle with her, and I certainly wasn't going to miss that opportunity! Her elder sibling, who had ridden up and down on my hospital bed some months before, was able to see my bald head, and we could tell her that I was starting to get better, but it might take a while.

Life felt extremely limited.
Before I came home, a group of ladies from Church kindly came and cleaned throughout the house for us and cleared away any out-of-date food from the fridge, as of course, Derek had rarely been there, and they made it as near to hospital cleanliness as possible. I had no appetite. And no energy. In hospital of course, I had had very little walking to do, and lived in a small, isolated room with an en-suite. Here, I could appreciate how far it was from my settee to the toilet! I had stairs to negotiate twice a day. Almost crawling up, Derek would walk behind me and help by quite literally pushing me as I held on to the bannister and took the weight on my arms. I had moved into the spare bedroom immediately after my first visit home and shared nothing, even with Derek, at that point.

Those days which proved worse than the days in hospital included days when I was physically incapable of getting up off the settee unaided. I needed someone around for a while. Not always necessarily needing to *do* anything other than be there, reading, knitting, answering their emails…! Company meant safety. Even if there was no talk. I was not alone with my thoughts for long periods of time.

I have already described my attempts to get up the stairs. The notion of having a bath was dismissed early on, when I realised, I couldn't get out. Showering was not possible as I had no strength in my legs to stand, and had no rails, as I do now. We encouraged people to arrange when to visit, and to check beforehand if I was up for it, and not to stay too long. I would be safely sitting on my settee, feet up, and sometimes able to chat for a while. I imagine some may have gone away thinking how well I was doing, without seeing me endeavour to move! I have done numerous home visits over the years, and never really thought beyond what I saw on the surface. This is something I have learned. Things are not always as they seem.

Going Out
But I did slowly recover. Having left the hospital in March and got accustomed to living at home, I reached the point when I dared to venture out of the house; initially hanging on to Derek, I walked from our front door to the neighbour's garage. Quite the achievement – and I felt very proud! I was on my way. From these small beginnings I gradually increased my distance while being taken for longer walks in a wheelchair. Derek was brilliant throughout all of this even though I'm sure I was quite difficult to live with at the time. The house had always been my "domain" while Derek was working; and now I could do nothing of any value and watched him getting more and more worn out. He would always deny being too tired, of course, no doubt wanting to protect me, but I could see it, even if he did think he was "Superman" sometimes! And when I did actually get back into things more, it was most frustrating, too, as things had been "moved"!

The first one hundred days were a big marker. As a recovering patient, my perspective was quite small compared to that of a healthy person. When I reached day 100, it was quite a landmark for me. It probably seemed insignificant to others. But I suppose it's a bit like asking a child who has just had their 8th birthday what it feels like to be eight. After all, they are only one day older! But to the child, who had possibly been looking forward to the occasion for weeks, if not months, it would be huge. For me day 100 signified a notable change: The pink envelope containing my funeral wishes was returned to me.

Rather like the day after the funeral of a loved one, after day 100, I started to look forward much more. Although my recovery was still slow and steady, I could glimpse a little normality returning to my life. For example, I remember my first venture out alone, with mobile in hand, keeping in touch with Derek, who was at work by this point, as I knew he would not relax until I was back at home. I had to remember - all by myself - to take my front door keys! I think it was in the June – ten months after diagnosis – that I made my first trip back to the Church I had been part of for almost thirty years, and that was very special. But also strange, as there were new faces and new songs, and I remember thinking "Some of these people may think I am a visitor!"

Starting Again

I made an attempt to return to teaching. Just one pupil to begin with (the others had either stopped or understandably found another teacher). The first lesson was great, and I recalled how much I loved my job. But after only 5 weeks, I realised even this was too much, as I never knew from one day to the next, how I was going to feel. This also coincided with needing a top-up of donor cells[9], so I stopped at that point and notified the tax office that I would no longer be working.

I struggled greatly with the thought of claiming benefit even though we needed it. What may seem a logical decision for an observer is often an emotional one for the person involved. It certainly was for me. Feelings of guilt crept in. Mostly because I was aware that there were so many people worse off than me. Add to that the sense that others may make

---

[9] The donor had donated some of his healthy cells, which were kept by for me in the hospital freezer. At this point, it seemed my system needed a little boost, so I was offered some more to top up those which had already become 'part of me'.

a judgement based on what they saw, The whole idea of claiming any help proved for me rather difficult. Maybe it shouldn't have, but that's how it was. Outwardly I looked like I was recovering; surely, I was well enough to resume work? I had a husband who was able to work. In my head I heard them saying 'They've almost certainly paid off their mortgage… (we hadn't)… they don't have any dependants… it doesn't seem right'.

Even as I write this, I realise the assumptions I made, and probably quite wrongly and unkindly, but my mind was in a turmoil about this for a long time. How often we assume we know what we don't. I sought advice about this from one of the leukaemia patients' advisors who asked whether I would still be working if it hadn't been for the leukaemia, a question which I could honestly answer in the affirmative. It had been my plan to work until at least the age of 70. So grudgingly, but very gratefully, I became the recipient of government help. As with the NHS, there are clearly huge challenges for the country in this area, but we are so fortunate to have the help we do in such times as these. In other places, Derek and I would have gone under. Totally bankrupt. Without our home. The costs involved in my care, in procedures, transfusions, tests, hospital bed and medication, were eye-wateringly high. We are so grateful.

By September 2015, I gradually started to attend Young at Heart again (the lovely group who had sent me the balloons and messages). Sue, who had taken over responsibility from me, and her team, had done wonders. The group had grown considerably, and they graciously allowed me to share in the leadership again, but without as much responsibility. This was just what I needed. It was good to feel useful again – more like 'me'.

Invisible
This has been one of the hardest things of all. Leukaemia is known as 'an invisible illness' – one of many such conditions. Due to this, there is often a lot of misunderstanding about it. What you see, with anyone, is not always the whole picture.

On the days when I went to Young at Heart, I seemed well, happy and back to almost as I was. And this was so, to a point. What might not have been apparent was that Monday would be spent resting up in preparation for the 2 hours the following morning. Tuesday afternoon I would be asleep in bed, and Wednesday was kept clear to recover.

My friends were so kind.

One might comment,

'Good to have you back'

Unfortunately, I would sometimes hear in my head,

'Good to have you back, let's get back to normal'

Another,

'Bet you're glad that's behind you now'

And I could hear,

'Bet you're glad that's behind you now. And you're fixed'

One might ask,

'Has your treatment all stopped now?'

Now this is a totally fair thing to ask. But inside me was a fear that I did not know if all the treatment had stopped or indeed if it ever would stop, in the long term. It looked that way at that moment, but anything could happen.

Rarer comments included such as,

'I see you aren't going to... *(an event)*... I thought you were better?'

I see now how this could simply have come from a desire to understand and support. I probably would have been the same, if I'm honest.

At the time, I just felt guilty that all wasn't 'normal'.

Me, Me, Me
A person with a long-term illness can certainly become very self-centred. I know I did at times. Sometimes I just couldn't seem to help it. I found myself expecting too much understanding from people which was totally unfair, because I was asking the impossible. Most of the time I could see that they were reaching out to me, showing their pleasure at me being there again, and being totally and utterly kind. But it has occurred to me because of experiencing this that I, and other people in similar situations to me, are in need of a lot of grace

and often forgiveness. And I certainly am. There is no right or wrong thing to say in this kind of situation as we are all so different. I have tried to outline some of the difficulties I have personally experienced, but others will have different reactions. And this I suppose is why we all need the forgiveness and the grace – on both sides – as we are negotiating a relationship with an illness 'intruder'. This is the thing. By around September 2015, life *had* resumed for me. In many ways, I *was* better; but many of the limitations I described at the beginning of the chapter remained.

One of the real highlights of this time was when we went to visit Jenny and family. I have a friend there with whom I sometimes go out for a coffee or lunch. We did this one day on a particular visit, to a place she had carefully chosen for safe spacing, as it was very early days for me going anywhere. We spent a lovely hour and a half or so, chatting as ladies are prone to do, and as I left the car after she drove me home, I remember thanking her for not talking about the leukaemia, as I realised that that had been a first for me since leaving hospital. Her answer was that she had been ready to talk or listen if I were to bring the subject up, and that the illness is something I "have" but it "doesn't define who I am." Back at home, it was always a topic of conversation, and to be fair, I had encouraged that as I hoped that openness was the best way for people to understand; and it was certainly better than having people not talking to me because they were worried about what to say, or whether I'd get upset if they talked about things I was no longer an active part of. And I realised that I was starting to think that way myself, as I couldn't yet fully see life past the illness. My feelings were all over the place, like a bowl of spaghetti, tangled up and messy. How did I feel? Half the time, I couldn't answer that question for myself let alone others. Maybe that's why we often resort to the time-honoured phrase "I'm fine thanks. You?"

Time and energy management

Activity uses up energy for each of us and it's not necessarily just physical. We tend to recognise the physical and respond accordingly. We exercise or do strenuous activity and get physically tired and this is a sign to us that we need rest. But there is also mental energy. Conversation can take a lot of mental energy either because of its length or its subject content. As can being sociable in any forum (particularly for the introvert). What about the emotional energy we use by conquering our fears or trying something for the first time? These are things I believe that are true of all of us, although I had never thought of it that way. Some activities, physical, mental or emotional, drain us and some refresh us.

My days were by now, after advice, planned on a traffic-light basis.

Red – a draining activity (in any of the above areas)

Green – a positively refreshing activity (maybe a hobby? Or a visit from a particular person?)

Amber – somewhere in between. Neutral, if you like.

One "red" activity a day was enough. And as I recovered more, each red activity needed to be balanced by a green one. Personally, I wonder if this wouldn't be a helpful guideline to anyone to help avoid the ever-increasing risk in our society of burnout.

The other thing I learned was that all days are not equal! Prior to my illness, overall, I could judge what I could do on any given day. I could look ahead, diary in front of me, and say

"Yes, next Thursday, I can do that, count me in."

Now I couldn't.

So, alongside the traffic light analogy, there were the batteries.

Some days began for me with a 75% battery (this was potentially a very good energy day)

Some days, it was clear from early on, that it was more like a 40% energy day.

Occasionally even less.

When I saw it like that it became obvious to me that I couldn't manage the same things on a 40% and 75% day. Why would I? The leukaemia advisor wisely pointed out to me that, in trying to get "back to normal", I was assuming that all the days were equal, and that was why I was often so frustrated with myself and my progress. This coupled with some others' misunderstanding. Yes, I was "better" in the comparative sense. But I was not "better" in that it was "back to normal." Learning to accept this was another great step forward.

The whole experience had changed me and the way I thought. My whole life plan had taken a U-turn overnight. Unexpected. Unavoidable. No warning. What's to stop this happening again? This concept that we carry as adults of "being in control" is tenuous to say the least! We are not in control at all. But I've come to believe that we can learn to take control within our limits.

There's that verse in the bible where Jesus says:

"I have come that they may have life, and have it to the full"

John 10:10 (NIV)

I struggled with this for a long time – it seemed somehow laughable given my circumstances – until I realised after much prayer that I *was* capable of this. There are people with a life-changing disability, living in a wheelchair for example, who live very fulfilling lives, and I also know of healthy people who do not. I *can* have life to the full. The beginning of another positive change of thinking for me. Much of which came through my own thought processes, praying, and sometimes worrying, but also having close friends I could talk to. 'A wise man has many counsellors' we are told, and I certainly found it to be true when on occasion I couldn't see the wood for the trees. From this time, I went forward with more of an acceptance of my daily battery level and any activity would be mentally measured on my traffic lights, and within that… yes, a full life.

Accepting each other

Why are we so often worried about others' perceptions? This was something I took much longer to come to terms with. I was, in the early days, quite defensive and I kept trying to explain why I did one thing, but not another, if anyone seemed genuinely interested. What I found fascinating, however, was that I could be asked one week e.g. if my treatment was now over, to which I would reply in the negative with an explanation of its longevity and open-endedness and have the same conversation with the same person a week later, and a week after that. I have since thought about this, and I realised (again!) that I would probably have been the same. We seem to have an innate need for finality. For everything to be alright. Maybe our brains find it difficult to compute too many ongoing situations. (And let's face it, I find it difficult enough and I am living it!) The freedom from this came much later, through the wise words of a friend, who challenged me about my concern. Why did I have to defend myself? Why *would* people be able to understand? How could they? How does a person who is happily married understand the agony of a divorce? Or the pain of a grieving wife or parent? There is no sense of blame when I say these things; I am simply trying to convey this part of my journey. It was unfair of me to expect others to understand what they cannot, and the way I struggled was more a reflection of my own need at the time to be understood. As time progressed, this need was met more and more through people at the Hospital Centre that I visited. What I needed at home was friends who were willing to just walk alongside me, and I am certainly blessed with those, and will always be grateful for their kindness and patience.

For the next two years or so, I continued the task of putting my life back together, rebuilding, and establishing the range of my abilities and limitations. Having come so far and learned so much, I began again to hope that there would now be a steady improvement in my health, and that I would as it was, go from strength to strength and become more involved with some of the activities that had come to a halt the previous year.

During this recovery time post-transplant, I continued to have regular checkups, as the doctors were keeping an eye on my blood levels. At first, they were quite often – I can't remember the specific timings, maybe weekly, fortnightly, then monthly? - then when my body seemed to be quite secure with my new bone marrow and I had stabilised, I was checked every three months. Wow, this felt like progress indeed! Finally, we reached the day in early 2017 when we were told to return in six months' time. To be totally honest, although I was aware this was a very good measure of my progress, there was also a level of anxiety and insecurity. Six months felt to me a very long time. When you've been watched so closely and have become accustomed to being given frequent updates that all was well, it felt a little bit like being cut adrift. I found I had become quite dependent on these reassurances. And a six-month wait till the next one felt like I was being told, 'You're on your own now… bye bye!'

I hasten to add that this was in no way true! At no point has that been the case. I just found it a little unnerving. I had a 24-hr telephone helpline. I could contact my local hospital, or Addenbrookes at any point that I was concerned. And of course, my recent experience was not common to all. It was far more usual for someone to live life assuming they were ok without having to be told so at regular intervals. It was another step to being healthy, so I made a decision - I would concentrate on being thankful for six months free of appointments and would simply enjoy it.

At some point in 2017, I had a very interesting experience. Functioning more independently at the time, I had driven myself to the local mini supermarket in the next village and felt fine. It was good to be useful again! Parking the car, I made my way to fetch a trolley for the task ahead. As you will probably be aware, the first stop in a supermarket is usually the fruit and veg, and I did not even get that far that day. The best way I can describe what happened that day is like this; imagine you had plugs in your feet which held in all your energy… and someone pulled the plugs out… all energy simply drained away… I sat down on the seat just inside the door and called Derek, who, not having the car of course, asked a friend to drive him over to get me home. I think I knew at that point, that something had changed. It was in fact an isolated incident, but as the Lord had done so many times throughout, I believe He provided me with time to mentally prepare for what was ahead.

Strangely, I have very little recollection of the appointments during this whole period. I had known the consultant at James Paget who made the initial diagnosis in 2014, and who had overseen my care throughout the hospital stays pre-transplant up to February 2015. Then there was another consultant, and I have absolutely no recollection of him at all. Derek has described the gentleman to me – but nothing. No memory at all. There were I assume, blood tests, but no feedback through face-to-face appointments.

My next memory was of being called to an unexpected appointment at the James Paget Hospital, before my six-month period had expired, where I was told that my blood levels had been 'drifting' over the last few tests, so they wanted some more done; and thus it transpired that there were early signs of leukaemic activity. Up until this point, I had been blissfully unaware of what was going on with me blood wise. It is largely because of this experience, where the doctors were aware of a gradual change of situation and I was not, that I started to request my results in more specific terms. However, despite lack of preparation in that way, I had the memory of the isolated incident at the local supermarket so when the doctor informed me in the August of 2017 that I was no longer in remission, I was able quite honestly to say that I was not at all surprised.

Jenny:

February 2016 (ish)
The unseen impact for me was what it was like at home, and by home, I now mean my home with my husband Sam in Derby. I think it was about 18 months after Mum's diagnosis (but I'm not sure on timeline, that's just what it is in my head) I looked around our home and said to Sam "this doesn't look like our home anymore." The term "cancer house" was then coined in our home to describe the way I felt about our home now. Sam had been absolutely marvellous and very supportive but there came a time when I had to start thinking more about my life in Derby and less about my life in Belton. That was very difficult for both of us. I had to spend some 2 months going through our home from top to bottom, not cleaning it as such, as "de-cancering" it. There were piles of stuff I had

been working on when Mum was diagnosed that I had shoved on a bookcase. Any paperwork received was in a box to be filed and there was a lot of it. There were notebooks with Mum's medication notes in that I hadn't referred to for months, but I still kept in my bedside table. Our cupboards were full of Sam's usuals when I wasn't there, or just pasta bakes for when I was. It was quite a cathartic experience and a very necessary one to look at our home and realise I had basically been bed-and-breakfasting there for over a year. Even when I had been at home, I hadn't really been there. I was either catching up on work, or catching up on sleep, or staring at a TV. Our marriage and our life together had kind of stopped in August 2014 and it took some time and a lot of work to start functioning as a couple again, and not just as occasional housemates.

It was also very hard for Sam because whilst he always understood any time I spent on Mum, or Dad or travelling, it was very difficult for him that keeping up with work was so important for me. I was driven by a few things – one was, that it was a quantifiable thing that I could see how I was doing and at a time where everything felt up in the air, the "number of hours behind/ahead" was a concrete figure and indicator of how I was doing, at a time when I didn't really know how I was doing. Also, if I fell behind, I felt like I had to catch up; partly because of my nature, and partly because of my employer's kindness in letting me work from home and not badgering me for hours etc. But even when I caught up (rare occasions!) I wanted to get ahead because of a "what if something happens next week" mentality. But it meant that for a long time, if there was a spare hour, it would go on work and not on my husband, even when I wasn't behind with work, and Sam got left behind.

It took us a while to get things back on track after that, and whilst I don't regret going back to my parents', and I don't regret working from there, and it all worked out in the end, if I have one regret it's that I was more worried about letting down my boss than I was letting down my husband, and I should have risked being behind with work to just be with him when I could be. I had seen what marriage looked like for my parents, and I didn't model it well myself. Fortunately, by the grace of God, by the time I was physically, emotionally and mentally back in Derby, Sam was still there waiting for me.

Derek and I had been married over thirty-five years by the time I was recovering from my transplant. We had had the usual ups and downs, of course, but never had we had to cope with a situation of this nature. When I read about Jen and Sam's experience it was heart breaking. Just to think that my misfortune had the potential to derail their marriage. I am just so thankful to God for bringing them through, and for Sam and his understanding and patience. He knows he is my favourite son-in-law, and that is only one of the reasons!

And George and Esther? On reading Esther's earlier reflection, I realise how my then 'soon-to-become-daughter-in-law' had every reason to resent me. Thankfully she chose not to. Whoever is married will know from experience that what affects one, will affect the other. The same will be true of each of my children, and like most mums, all I want to do is make it better. And I am not able to.

Sue B:

When Jane was diagnosed with Leukaemia the Church was praying for her, myself included. One day as I was reading my Bible in the Gospel of John chapter 11 part of verse 4 jumped out at me. It read "This sickness will not end in death." The thought immediately came to me "This means Jane." I kept this to myself for many months in case it was just my wishful thinking. I continued praying for Jane. Months later I mentioned my thoughts to Tim our Vicar's husband. He asked me if I had told Jane. I said I hadn't as I didn't want to give her false hope in case it was just my own thoughts. However, he thought I should tell her. After praying again, I eventually told her the words that had come to me that day. Jane has now survived for 9 years and 2 bone marrow transplants so I can only assume that God put those words into my mind that day. Praise His Name.

I was very grateful that Sue waited her time to share what she felt was an answer to her prayer for me. I was also pleased that she had another opinion at that point. It is my understanding (and Sue's), that none of us can be 100% sure when we have such a thought, and as with so many things in life, I suppose, I say to myself, 'time will tell'. Having said that, it was a great encouragement to me. Because it gave me another reassurance that God was in this in so many ways, even though I didn't know for sure exactly how, or what the outcome would be. So, at the time, I held it lightly, although as many years have since gone by, I can't help but begin to wonder. Certainly, so far, it has proved to be the case, otherwise I wouldn't be writing this! I have heard it said that having a faith in God makes life easier. In many ways I would agree, although if I'm honest, there are times when it can add a bit of confusion to the proceedings. Another layer of unknowns.

Adjustments

Our speaker in Church one day talked briefly about the Bible story known as the Exodus. The Israelites had been living as slaves in Egypt for around 400 years, at which point, under the leadership of Moses, they were set free. The whole story can be found in the 2nd book of the Bible. The point made in the talk was that it then took about 40 years of preparation before they could even consider functioning as an independent people. They retained the 'slave mentality' for quite a while. Moses could 'take Israel out of Egypt' but taking 'Egypt out of Israel' was a different story entirely.

There followed a present-day example regarding modern slavery. The International Justice Mission (IJM) and other similar organisations are working constantly to free people from all forms of modern slavery conditions. Their task of achieving freedom for the slaves, difficult enough in itself, does not end at point of release; there follows of necessity a restorative programme of adjustment – acclimatisation to a life of independence. A slave may have been freed in all practical, external terms, but the internal mentality from slave to free-thinking person takes some considerable time.

Throughout my story, I speak of certain adjustments I felt I needed to make in response to changes in my external situation. Initially it was simply from that of a healthy, full life, to one more confined. There followed the frequent and sometimes quite sudden changes from feeling reasonably ok, to feeling downright ill. The whole concept of change in any situation seems to challenge many of us. Or is that just me? We seem to like what we know to some degree. It made me wonder whether this was what God always intended for us. Strangely, I perceive that even in the natural world around us, nothing stays the same. A flower which was in bud on Tuesday is in full bloom by Friday. The grass was short (it feels like only yesterday!) and now it needs cutting again. Those trousers were long enough for my 9-yr-old son last week, now they are shin-high. Change is inbuilt into any vibrant life.

The challenges I faced it seems were, and are, far more linked with my internal responses. My attitudes and expectations. My adaptability. I like certain changes (a wage-rise perhaps? A less harsh work schedule? Feeling healthier?). I like these sort of changes as they provoke a pleasurable response. They help me to feel happy and content. No problem with those changes whatsoever! However, when the change is not perceived by me to be to my advantage, ('oh no, it's raining and I had planned a barbecue' or 'I feel worse today'), it's a different story. So maybe, just maybe, it's not the change itself that bothers me overall, but rather I just don't like being disturbed from my routine, or simply being disappointed. I like to be in charge. I like it my way. A challenging thought.

In the television series, "The Big Bang Theory" there is a character called Sheldon who hates anything that disturbs his totally planned and routine life. (Spoiler alert! The next few lines reflect a portion of the penultimate episode). Averse to change of any kind, Sheldon is faced with a considerable amount after he, along with his wife, won the Nobel Prize.

His wife has a makeover and looks very glamorous.

As they leave their apartment block, they are confronted by a noisy group of reporters.

He receives a standing ovation on his first subsequent visit to the canteen.

He is approached for interviews.

Whilst talking it over with a friend, his comment was simply,

'All this change? It's just too much…'

But what really struck me was the subsequent interaction:

Friend: 'I guess the only thing that actually stays the same is that things are always changing.'

Sheldon: 'So, the inevitability of change might be a universal constant…'

To me that makes sense.

Change of some form will inevitably take place – my only choice is how I deal with it.

Before: On holiday in Germany the previous June and coffee with Jane P.

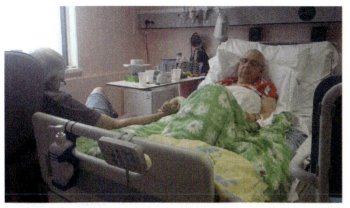

During: At various stages of treatment

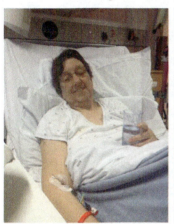

George & Esther's Wedding: A special day

After: Our family together
(Christmas season 2014 and early 2019 respectively)

Meeting the babies:
Abi, 2015
Katie, 2018
Ben, 2020
(Cuddles with Ben had to wait)

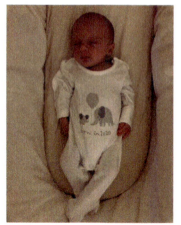

Grandchildren:
Jess aged 4.
(Our only grandchild at time of diagnosis)

Ben, Katie,
Abi & Jess in 2023

CHAPTER 6:
AND IT'S BACK: AUGUST 2017

> **Song:**
> 'Praise You in this storm' by Casting Crowns

I had been aware from Day One that there was always a chance that the leukaemia might re-emerge. Originally, I had been told if this were the case, I would be put back on chemo, but this time with a view to keeping the disease at bay as long as possible. There are new treatments coming along all the time, they said. They wouldn't give up on me. After all, they had 'known people to live for up to two years' after such a relapse.

I had got my head round this as much as anyone can, I think, and I was prepared to be told more details at my upcoming appointment. I was now, as I thought of it, "on a clock." Of course, all of us are, but for the most part, I imagine we don't in the normal run of things daily ponder how long we have left on earth, until we are considerably older. Certainly pre-August 2014, I had assumed (rather presumptuously!) that I would live well into my eighties at least. My mum was very active and involved in life until she died at the age of 92. My maternal Nan was in her late eighties. I had been fit and healthy… well, maybe not "fit" exactly, but certainly well and active. And I was only 57 at the time. Such thoughts simply had not been there at that point.

When it started to look like I was relapsing in 2017, I understood that the chemo offered at this point would have a different purpose. Chemotherapy itself is toxic. It is designed to kill off the leukaemic cells and thus crush the disease. The flip side of this is that simultaneously, healthy cells are destroyed too. This is why patients on chemo treatment feel so poorly, and why they need time to recover and blood levels to be restored[10] before the next lot of treatment is given – which knocks you back again. And because it stays in your body for ages afterwards you are always fighting the effects of the chemo as well as any infections you may get. It is rough. But what is staggering is how far research has come, enabling scientists to produce quite individual personalised treatment. How thankful we must be for this.

In the light of all this now, if the leukaemia had indeed returned, the purpose of the chemo would be to try to keep the disease under control for as long as possible. Of course, the fact remains that chemotherapy itself does damage to both healthy and diseased cells. But if the positive effects of it outweighed the negative ones, I would continue as an outpatient, living my life with as many or few precautions as I chose to take, on a cycle of seven daily appointments out of every month. So, my thinking turned to:

1. One week and two days of chemo
2. Approximately one week recovery time
3. Two weeks of enjoying / living life

This way of thinking inevitably makes one think about their priorities in life.

What really matters at the end of the day?

How much time do I waste?

How can I use my time well, to the best advantage?

I would continue with this pattern, and they would treat any subsequent infections with antibiotics, until such times as

1. The chemo stopped working.
2. I got an infection that we couldn't beat.
3. The chemo gets too bad and I had had enough.

I've often heard it said that sometimes the treatment is worse than the disease. I sort of get that now. If you are in pain with

---

[10] I explained earlier that the elements in the blood are measured through regular blood tests. These results are recorded, often in the form of a graph, so we can see the trend. Is the graph line staying steady? Or rising or falling? Platelets for example might be gradually diminishing in number, flagging up the concern of excessive bleeding due to the inability of the blood to clot safely.

an arthritic hip, for example, although there is pain after a hip replacement, I have been told it is a different sort of pain. And of course, that should be temporary as it improves daily, and there is an end in sight. Something to look ahead to – a day of being pain-free if all goes well. Previously, when my transplant took place, I had had chemotherapy to kill off all my diseased bone marrow cells. These had then been replaced by healthy cells kindly donated by my donor. But this time the healthy part of me would deteriorate with no total replacement, although a top-up of donor cells could be given if appropriate.

With leukaemia, and other illnesses like it, I imagine, there seems to be some truth in the original claim that sometimes the treatment is worse than the disease. Or maybe it just seems that way? Many times, I have attended an appointment and on being asked how I was feeling, would answer that I was feeling quite well, thank you, until after you've got your hands on me!

A steadying influence

Throughout all of this, the treatment and the rollercoaster of emotional adjustments that needed to be made regularly, God was there alongside. Friends, family and many Church congregations continued to pray for me and supported me in other ways. My prayers for myself have never been for healing and I wondered why this was. On reflection, I think it has been because, although I have no doubt in my mind that God is capable of wiping out diseases, I am also aware that this is not always (I might even say comparatively rarely?) the case. But I know from His Word that He always answers prayers and gives us our deepest need. I've never been a particularly volatile person, swinging from extremes of high to low mood (although like everyone, I've had my moments!) - in the light of the path I was now walking I was aware that I needed a steadying influence to keep me on an even keel, as it were, and for me, God provided that. I prayed that I would know and feel His presence with me throughout. That He would prepare me for whatever I would hear in any given appointment… for what was coming next. That He would help me with adjusting to the ever-changing circumstances of my life. And He has answered these prayers. To this I can wholeheartedly testify. I have always known the score and have had to learn to live each day as it comes to the best of my ability. Maybe Jesus had a point, when considering the many things we fret about, "Seek first His (God's) Kingdom and His righteousness and all these things will be given to you as well. Therefore, do not worry about tomorrow for tomorrow will worry about itself. Each day has enough trouble of its own" (Matthew 6 v.33 NIV). I wish I could say I was always successful in trusting this, but that would be a lie. However, I am improving.

There were, and still are, low days. Sometimes, Derek or I, for no apparent reason will be sad or tearful. Sometimes unusually snappy with each other. We are learning to say openly "It's just one of those days when it is all simply too much" We've learned to accept these days for what they are and not to fight them and generally it gets better by the following day.

A new insight
We went to the New Wine Christian Conference earlier that same year, 2017, opting to stay in a hotel instead of camping. Being very aware of what news might be waiting for me back home, I attended a fascinating seminar. The speaker's talk was entitled "Through despair into joy" He too had had a traumatic diagnosis of cancer. It was a different cancer from mine, but there was a startling similarity in the speed in which his life was turned upside down. He described his situation as a grief.

Grief? This was a further moment of revelation for me, this explained exactly what and how I was feeling. And I had already learned through the experience of life, that grief after bereavement was not to be avoided or suppressed but to be lived through and in the very process of grieving there can come healing. But, I had argued with myself, no-one had died… But I realised I grieved over:
1. The life I had previously and had lost.
2. The future I had planned.
3. The hopes and dreams I had held dear,
    e.g. I had always wanted to be a 'hands-on' nanny like my Mum had been to my children. I would be able to

give my children, when parents, a haven of much needed rest from time to time.
4. My loss of independence.
5. My lack of security.
6. My inability to plan ahead.

There were more. And more are coming to light as time has gone on. So much made sense. No person had died, but many hopes and dreams had. My career had. My ministry as it was had come to a sudden end. As I sat in this seminar, I knew I was to hear on my return home to Belton, what the future held for me regarding the reoccurrence of the leukaemia. It was 99% certain in my mind, but as so often, it was not fully known. I was very much in limbo.

At the same conference… before or after, I don't recall which, I attended another talk at the end of which there was an opportunity for prayer ministry[11]. The details of the talk are sketchy to say the least, but the focus for prayer was the idea of stepping into a flowing river; ankle deep, knee deep, waist deep; eventually so deep that one had to swim. It was about moving in faith into the unknown. About trusting God. I do however remember distinctly two things. I was scared to even move from where I was into the unknown, scared to even get 'in the water' as it were. I also recall I never spoke a word. I certainly didn't want to have to go into detail with a complete stranger in that situation. I was outwardly holding myself in check, being very 'brave' (ha-ha!) but inside me I was crying out for some help, somehow. During my silence I was simply saying to God, I can't do this, won't You just carry me? I knew I feared what was coming. I couldn't move forward on my own. Not a word was spoken aloud by me. The lady who was praying with me however, spoke after a few moments and said she didn't know if this would mean anything to me, but she had had a strong picture as she prayed, of me being picked up and carried into the river as I hadn't the strength to do it on

---

[11] This is where someone will pray for the specific need of another as requested.

my own. That was when I cried. I had my reassurance of God's presence, yet again.

As I processed these things with God in prayer, I realised God would have a new plan for me, in His time.

And I would find it.

I would.

He had taken me this far.

He was not going to stop now.

Why would He?

Derek:

Sometimes when I feel God speak to me, I write what He says in an email to myself. I was out walking and praying when I asked God a question. I emailed the conversation to myself the next morning and repeated it the next day.

> Date: Thu, August 10, 2017, 06:48
> Subject: Question
>
> I asked the question is it back? Yes
> Will You stop it? No
> Are we in for a tough time? Yes
>
> As you can imagine this came as quite a shock. The following day I repeated back to God what I had asked previously and the same responses,
>
> Yesterday I asked the question is it back? And You replied, "Yes."
>
> I heard, "That is correct."
>
> I asked, "Will you stop it?" and You replied "No."
>
> I then asked, "Are we in for a tough time?" and You answered "Yes."
>
> Tears running down my face, I then added, "Will the doctors be able to do anything?"
>
> And I believe I heard You say, and this was the gentle tone of voice, "Ah, now that's a different question."
>
> A little later I heard, "You will be amazed at what the doctors can do."

And I, we, have been.
A few days later we were told the leukaemia was back.

Rosie:

Something that is difficult to write is that God motivated the church to pray for Jane; faith was tested; doubts raised by a few people "how could God let Jane suffer in this way" with the suggestion that good people shouldn't suffer. Some difficult conversations about suffering led me to revisit it in my reading and thinking, strengthening my understanding that God doesn't send sickness, that He travels with us through the distress and pain of ill-health; that He aids us in all ways – but not always how and when we want Him to.

Difficult times within the church at the same time as Jane being so ill. Jane's desire for us to pray for the church as well as for Jane herself – such a gracious act, and I am so thankful for her love and care of the church family, as they were/are of her. As it should be – we rejoice together, we mourn and are sad together, but most of all we stick together. So thankful for God-given/inspired unity at that time.

Pat:

I remember talking with you when it hit you again – about whether or not you were going to go through all that again. So glad you and your family made the decision you did.

CHAPTER 7:
WHAT DO WE DO NOW?

We returned home to Belton in that August of 2017, having enjoyed the New Wine Conference, to the confirmation that leukaemic activity had indeed begun again as we had expected. So, it was real. We began adjusting - again - to our different pattern of life. This now included seven consecutive days (excluding weekends) of daily injections per month. Three injections a day. Twenty-one during each course of treatment. In practice it meant that one full week and two Mondays and Tuesdays every month were 'taken' as it were, but for the other three weeks we were mostly free of hospital appointments. This all came into play from August of 2017.

Being on chemotherapy, I was again more vulnerable to infection, so earlier rules regarding meeting people, food limitations and general infection avoidance were resurrected. After the first transplant back in 2015, Derek and I had increasingly become adjusted to our new way of life, thankful for our 'second chance' if you like. Being aware of God's part in it all and looking ahead in the hope that I had been "cured", I certainly was by this time acutely aware of time passing. There were good and not-so-good appointments and mostly good results and we had been looking ahead in the hope of reaching the longed-for 5-year mark. (If one stays in remission for 5 years, experience has shown that recurrence is much less likely. Not impossible, but a greatly reduced likelihood).

Partially prepared through the New Wine Conference and the previous experience at the supermarket, I now knew it to be a fact. After two and a half years my blood levels had indeed dropped and a bone marrow test had confirmed that the leukaemia was active again. It was happening. But, God had prepared me - us. We knew what was coming. We were ready. Or were we?

Surprises ahead

At the meeting with our transplant consultant in 2017 the two options were outlined to us.

A regular dose of chemo aimed to keep on top of the disease, as I had been told originally.

Or a second transplant.

What? This was a total surprise. Well, to be honest, more of a shock! There had been no preparation from the doctors regarding this possibility. When we queried this, it was explained to us that, at the time of the previous discussion some time back, NHS funding for second transplants in the case of relapse had been stopped. So, at that point, I had been told correctly. And I don't know the timeframe exactly, but after much lobbying from Leukaemia charities and probably other interested parties, the availability of NHS-funded second transplants was reinstated. A real turn around. Providing me, and others in a similar situation, with another chance to overcome the disease.

But by now, I was sixty-one years old, and therefore surely too old for this to even be considered as a feasible proposition? However, we were told that day that, as I had responded well to the treatment, and was still a relatively well and active person, I would be offered one. Doctors are, I believe, not allowed (or maybe not encouraged?) to give advice on what a patient ought to do. At the end of the day the decisions are up to the patient. Personally, I find this quite difficult as I grew up believing that doctors were the experts, and they knew best and I would have been more than happy just to do what I was told. But now I faced this huge decision. The consultants throughout though have been amazing. We were able to speak openly and honestly, knowing they pull no punches. I could ask anything. From what I remember that day, my question was something like 'I know you can't tell me what to do, and I'm not asking you to; I understand it is my decision, but…' As a result of the ensuing conversation, I came to realise that although as in all these situations there is a risk involved, it was my only chance of an actual cure. Why might it work for me this time, when it hadn't before? Was hitting my body harder with chemotherapy (which is how it was described to me) even possible?

> **Song:**
> 'It is well with my soul' by Matt Redman

Decisions

My children, now grown-up and constantly supportive, on hearing this all turned up at our house on the Friday evening. I continue to be stunned and somewhat humbled by that. More love shown in action. We spent time sharing all our thoughts and desires. I openly told them that I dreaded the thought of going through a second transplant and didn't know that I could face it. I had told the rector, who in turn told the Church, and asked that they respect our need for privacy as we made this decision. And I am sure it will have prompted some to pray for us that weekend, giving us more much-needed support.

As our family talked that weekend, each said to me that they wanted me to consider having the second transplant, but that they would support any decision Derek and I made.

No guilt.

No coercion.

No expectation.

Just a sharing of thoughts and utter support. What a blessed mother and wife I am indeed. We prayed together and they left us with it. By the Tuesday, I sent the message to the hospital – and my family – that I would go ahead.

I told myself this time I was more prepared. I knew what was coming, I knew what I needed in the way of nighties, dressing gown, duvet, and other such personal items. I knew what activities I could take with me, what I was likely to feel well enough to do. I packed lots of notelets on which to write to people as I had before; I took puzzles, books and colourings, my holding cross and a bible. Rosie, knowing I like to paint, had kindly bought me watercolour brushes for use with watercolour pencils, ideal for use in a hospital bed. Derek knew the set-up with the flat. He knew what meals were easy to prepare. He had an idea of what was needed in this situation. Yes, we were all set.

Jenny would help where she could, as she had before, but maybe not quite in the same way as by now she was in the early stages of pregnancy along with the associated sickness. Why they call it morning sickness is a mystery to me as my experience was not limited to a specific time of day – and I don't think Jenny's was either! I'll never know how she managed to hold it all together when she visited, especially when it was a toss-up which one of us was the more nauseous!

So, although from initially not being at all prepared for the possibility of a second transplant, yet again, I had made the necessary adjustments in my thinking and I was now as ready as I could be. I'd done it before – and I was more prepared practically this time round. Despite still being scared at the thought, I knew God was with me and wouldn't let me down. Bring it on. With the matter settled in my mind, I set about this interim period of waiting for the new transplant date to come around.

Same, but different

During this period August 2017-May 2018, in many ways things outside of hospital continued much as they had done, but on a more scheduled pattern. I learned to organise my activities around the chemotherapy schedule. It proved to be an easy programme of treatment in comparison with what I had experienced before. Life did not come to a standstill this time, it simply needed to be rearranged. I could do less, but I could do something! I remember feeling very grateful for this.

At the Sandra Chapman Centre however, I was back to being a 'regular', and again I would strike up conversations with other patients, a few known to me, but mostly newer additions. This was interesting too, in that I was now an 'old hand', and found myself not so much someone in need of information or assurance from others, so much as the encourager. I knew where the kitchen was - I could show where things were kept – I knew when the tea trolley was expected to turn up, and what was usually on offer for dinner on any given day! Sometimes I would see a shadow pass over someone's face when I answered their inevitable question, 'how long have you been coming here?' - as they began to consider the possibility that their illness might not necessarily be short term, as I had previously needed to do. But I also saw (or maybe I just imagined?) glimmers of hope from time to time, when they could see that I had undergone the transplant experience - which was still a scary unknown in their future - and I was sat right there in front them. It was true that I needed treatment again, but I had come through the procedure, and was still around. This shift in position, if you like, was of interest to me. I had previously sought out people 'ahead of me' in the journey. As time passed, I found them to be fewer and fewer.

So here I was, in 2017, undergoing treatment in preparation for the second transplant. As ready as I could possibly be. However, as with so many of the best laid plans in life, it turned out to be a totally different experience altogether.

CHAPTER 8:
SECOND TIME ROUND: MAY 2018

From arrival at Addenbrookes at the end of May ready for the second transplant, it felt different. Maybe it always is different, simply because it is the second time. Life, it seems, doesn't tend to repeat itself exactly (maybe because *we* are different due to the previous experience). This time, some members of staff were different, and treatments and methods had moved on. Staff pressures would be different – unbeknown to me of course, as they rarely gave a hint of pressure, beyond the occasional comments, 'we're a bit short-staffed today', 'it was a long night' or 'everything seems to happen all at once'.

Then of course, there was the inevitable 'Well, you don't need me to tell you that, you've been here before, so you know the ropes'. Were their expectations of me higher this time round? Were mine too low? Did I just imagine that? I certainly *had* changed. I had come a long way from my initial mind-set of the notion 'I'm ill, I get treated, and I get back to normal'- Well past it! This time it was more in the mental climate of

'What have I let myself in for?'

'How will I cope if it is worse?'

'Should I find it easier to deal with because I know what's coming?'

'Will it work this time?

'If it does, it might give me more time with my grandchildren',

'Will it be more difficult to leave grandchildren 8 and 3 years of age, rather than regret missing any not yet born?'

Looking back

At the time of my first transplant in February 2015, one daughter-in-law was expecting a baby. It was unknown to me whether I would ever meet him/her, and it was a huge moment for me when I did. How excited I had been – albeit in a rather dopey sort of way!

This time round, Jenny had told me very early on that she was pregnant, for me to have something to look forward to, and of course, I did. It is the most natural thing to be excited about the birth of a grandchild. But on hearing the news I made an almost immediate decision not to dwell too much on this, not to go down the road of high expectation or anticipation. I would previously have looked forward to supporting my daughter in pregnancy and certainly in the early days/weeks especially with a first child. But this time, I simply could not allow myself to become too engaged with the possibility that it might occur. I feel bad about this sometimes and maybe I did miss out on an exciting time of anticipation – but I genuinely didn't think I could cope with the sheer disappointment of it not transpiring. So, I chose not to get my hopes up. I've thought about this, and other similar situations in terms of getting a subject or worry 'out of its box' for a little while – enjoying it, or dealing with it, then returning it to its safe place in my brain. I was glad I knew, and the thought of being a Nanny again was lovely, but I didn't get my hopes up any more than I needed to. All through, I have prayed that God would do the preparing for me, so I would be ready at the appropriate time for any eventuality, and He has. I continued to live on that basis. One day at a time.

When I missed our younger son's wedding, there had never been any real chance of me attending, as it was during the time I was in and out of hospital on aggressive pre-transplant chemo, and a good day was symbolised by being able to walk from hospital bed to toilet and back. Being allowed out for the day, watching online from home, and those few precious photographs was all for me beyond my wildest dreams. With Jenny's pregnancy it was different. The transplant was imminent (end of May) while the baby was due in December or January. So, there were different possible outcomes. I think in retrospect that's why I shut them down in my mind and assumed the worst – I wouldn't be part of it – and anything above that would be a bonus.

My reality now

My first surprise after hospital admission was being taken down to have a tube put into my stomach to feed me. This had not happened last time. They told me it was standard practice with second transplants due to the tougher chemotherapy. I would feel more ill and this would take the pressure away from me regarding the need to eat. Added to the lack of desire to eat and accompanying nausea, were the large blister-like sores I had in my mouth and on my lips making everything near my mouth painful. I was able to have oral morphine before attempting to eat, but I was particularly grateful that there was a freezer near the ward where we could stash away icepops, which day or night I could request and the cold from them brought me some temporary relief. I had never had an endoscopy or tube down my throat for any reason, so naturally I was a little nervous. Actually, very nervous. This was another occasion when I was extremely thankful for the calm assurance of the nursing staff and even more deeply that of God. As I was wheeled back up to the ward after the procedure, I did feel a little uncomfortable (and I always felt as if my nose was running!) but I felt genuine relief that food would be less of an issue than last time round. At least initially.

My fluid intake (and output) was, as before, watched and measured closely and I was constantly being nagged about needing to drink more. And getting tablets down me was a real source of what I can only describe as dread. Staff came in in the morning with their cocktail of tablets – between twelve and fifteen of them – and these could take all morning for me to manage and I often couldn't keep them down. There were fewer at lunchtime, then a further bulk arrival at teatime. Fewer again at night. At one point they told me apologetically that they only had in stock the smaller dosage of one of the pills (e.g. 50mg rather than 200mg) This may seem on the face of it a small problem I imagine, but for those few days, I would need 4 x small tablets instead of the one, my total number of daily tablet intake temporarily increasing to 45. This is etched on my memory as a period of horror. I was taking a tablet with a few sips of water approximately every fifteen minutes and was still expected to have a drink in between. That coupled with the persistent diarrhoea and vomiting kept my fluid levels low and was a constant challenge to me and I'm sure, a frustration to the nursing staff!

My chemo this time came in the form of an intravenous drip two or three times a day for four days. This was followed by a "chemo holiday" of two days, culminating in four more days' treatment prior to transplant day. Meaning eight days of chemo in the ten-day period. There was, it seemed, a cumulative effect on my body: the more chemo went in, the worse I felt. I was doing very little as I recall, despite all my well-planned activities, I could do nowhere near as much as I'd been able to do three years earlier. I tried to crochet some squares for a baby blanket. Jenny had provided me with a worship song to hear each day, complete with the written words. Some days I couldn't even listen to them if I needed to find them myself.

I didn't want to read.

I didn't even know the TV in my room didn't work until the engineer came along to fix it. Derek would read my texts aloud to me (keeping me loosely in contact with that 'outside world'). He read a story from "Just William" to me at night to help me to relax before sleeping and it became a bit of a joke that I had to hear the same story many times as I rarely stayed awake to the end. This simple act of reading to me was really comforting and I so looked forward to this time. He was very patient with me. Outside of these glimmers of enjoyment, this was indeed the darkest three weeks of the whole time.

From bed to bedside commode.

Feeling more ill than I knew possible, coupled with the emotions and questions….is this all worth it?

By chemo day seven, the nurse hooked up the bag as usual and I was desperate. I looked straight at her and asked, "Do I *have to*?" I just wanted to cry. I may well have done so, as I was past caring about that. I remember to this day, her kindness. She simply waited, and when I was ready to hear, she said "I'll just pop the bag up, shall I? We'll try it. I can always stop it if you want me to. And tomorrow *is* the last day" I agreed. It sounded so reasonable amid my confusion. And that was enough. But in my heart of hearts, I knew I was ready to give in at that point had I been given any encouragement to do so. This was new to me. I'd never felt that way before. I had had enough, and putting aside family and friends, I wanted to quit.

Where was God now?

Where was God in all this? He was so close to me the first-time round. Prayer had been a joy. A blessing. A way of being useful in a time of seeming uselessness (as I saw it to be then). Now all was dark. Now, it seemed, God was silent. A dark three weeks. Words of prayers hit the proverbial 'wall' and I felt as if I might as well speak into a tin can for all the good it was doing.

The fourth verse of an old hymn became very important to me at this time. I would say the words in my head or sometimes out loud, over and over again.

> Dear Lord and Father of mankind,
> forgive our foolish ways!
> Re-clothe us in our rightful mind,
> in purer lives thy service find,
> in deeper reverence, praise;
> in deeper reverence, praise.
>
> In simple trust like theirs who heard,
> beside the Syrian sea,
> the gracious calling of the Lord,
> let us, like them, without a word,
> rise up and follow thee;
> rise up and follow thee.
>
> O Sabbath rest by Galilee!
> O calm of hills above,
> where Jesus knelt to share with thee
> the silence of eternity
> interpreted by love!
> interpreted by love!
>
> Drop thy still dews of quietness,
> till all our strivings cease;
> take from our souls the strain and stress,

and let our ordered lives confess
the beauty of thy peace;
the beauty of thy peace.

Breathe through the heats of our desire
thy coolness and thy balm;
let sense be dumb, let flesh retire;
speak through the earthquake, wind, and fire,

O still, small voice of calm;
O still, small voice of calm.

John G Whittier

Why this hymn? It was not a regular at our Church at the time, although I did know it from when I was younger. It was the only "prayer" I could pray. I individualised the words so that I was singing simply about me, over and over. Sometimes I would continue to the last verse if I could recall the words.

During this time, during these dark three weeks, on one of my particularly bad vomiting periods, I coughed up my tube (I had asked about this possibility when they put it in, 'oh no!' they had said, 'even being sick won't fetch it out'……seems they were mistaken!) Fortunately, Derek was with me, and although it was a bit scary at the time, it was easily dealt with. It did however mean that I had to have another one inserted as I was not yet able to eat independently and had only managed nutritional drinks.

I was getting quite frustrated about feeling so distant from God. I had often previously testified to people about how God had carried me through until now. And I stood by that – still do. Initially I was in my bubble. This time round, it felt as if I was totally on my own.

Was it a test of faith?

Was I not being faithful in some way?

Was I doing something wrong?

Oh, the times people have said similar things to me in the past and I have given an answer – maybe a true one, but not at all empathetic – 'God is always with you. Just trust. He has promised it.' I was realising now that these words probably meant diddly-squit to them as much as they did to me at that moment.

What I really craved was someone just telling me I was doing ok.

To assure me I was safe.

Someone who stood alongside and understood.

I needed to be reminded that others would take this burden of worry and pray on my behalf, and I could just rest and wait on God. Maybe I was told exactly this, but I was so convinced that I must have been doing something wrong to prevent God becoming close, I doubt I could have heard it at that point anyway. Sometimes I think, we all must simply pray and wait on God. Maybe there are occasions when others' words are just not enough. Only a word or touch from God will be of any help.

I started to see
And that hymn verse, my prayer at this time, was I see now, very indicative of how "in control" and "ready" I had wanted to be in practical terms for this second stay at Addenbrookes. I can almost hear God saying with a smile , 'Oh, yeah… and where's *that* got you?' I can smile at the stupidity of it now too, but it wasn't funny at the time. At the height of my frustration and the depth of my despair, I had one of the greatest experiences of God I have ever had. Wanting to be in control of course, meant that I was trying to be strong. Trying to show how faithful I could be.

Trying. Trying. Trying.

And failing.

Why was it so difficult?

So, I turned on God and accused Him of not being there.

Why was He not responding?

Why has He left me alone like this?

At that very moment I 'saw' a silhouette at the foot of my bed. I cannot prove of course, whether it was my mind playing tricks – wishful thinking – or whether it was God-given reassurance, but it had never happened before and hasn't in that way since, so I tend to go with the God-given option. Him saying to me, in effect, I am here. The silhouette was in clear profile. There were no details or features, just a presence. Then I let it all out.

"Well, if You are here why aren't you listening to me?"

I was angry. I've thought since that maybe it was a bit like the psalmists of old, when they ranted at God about different situations. Normally, I think I may be too 'polite' to let go in this way.

His answer?

'I am listening. You are not talking to Me.'

That was like a red rag to a bull.

"I am talking to you! Or trying to, at least. All the time!"

And the quiet response.

"But you are not telling me how you *really* feel"

At that point, I know I cried. There alone in the room, I cried and poured it all out. The truth. I hated it there.

I wanted to go home.

I'd never get better if I stayed there.

I couldn't eat.

I never wanted food at the right time.

I'd had enough.

I wanted to go home.

And there it was. The truth was finally spoken.

And then, whichever side of the bed I looked, in whichever direction, there was that silhouette. All around, everywhere I looked. And just like that, the awareness of God's presence was re-established. He had always been with me even though I'd lost sight of that, but now I knew it again.

Nothing on the surface had changed.

I still felt rough.

Still couldn't eat.

Still hated it all.

But now I knew I was not alone.

God was still in it all and again I felt His peace.

Song:
'You already know' by J.J. Heller

Unseen Certainties

My brother has a first-class degree in Chemistry. He also understood a fair bit of physics. I do not share that ability! In fact, the night before sitting these two obligatory science GCE 'O' levels years ago, I remember being still totally flummoxed, and he sat me down and said '*If you get a question mentioning a and b, use this formula. If it mentions c and d, use this one…*' The list continued. (I don't recommend this method!) When I scraped a pass with a level 6 in each subject, he actually asked me if I'd not misread it when it should have been a 9!

Why do I tell you this? Simply because when Rob, my eldest, was very young, he showed a great interest in all things way outside of my understanding. And he never let up with the questions!

How? Why? Where?

One day he asked me – yet again - how the light in our living room worked.

What *is* electricity?

How does it work?

I walked him to the switch, and gave the following explanation:

'Look, Rob. The fact is I don't know.

See this switch?

I turn it on.

The light comes on.

This happens through electricity.

If the light doesn't come on, I ask your dad.

That is the extent of my knowledge.

You'll just have to ask someone else about this'.

Electricity? I still can't understand or explain it.

But I *know* it's there because something happens when I press that switch.

When I experienced what I called the 'silhouette' which appeared in my mind's eye around that hospital bed as I was praying, I didn't understand it. Still don't. I couldn't explain it. Still can't. But I know something happened. Something changed from that time. I just *knew*. I felt different. Have you ever experienced a 'look' someone gives you, where no words are spoken, but the look speaks volumes for itself? It can't be explained. But you just *know*. (Parents and teachers are particularly adept at this!) Or whilst going out with someone as a friend, and then one day there's something – a look, a touch, a gesture – from which you just *know* you are no longer simply friends. Nothing has been said. But from that point there is an unspoken understanding between you. Or a look which passes between two people while witnessing something potentially dangerous, which shows a knowing concern only born out of shared experience or wisdom. Nothing needs to be said.

We humans are very complicated beings. There are levels to our understanding that we respond to subconsciously, but can't really explain with words:

Instincts.

Body language.

Looks.

Gestures.

Sighs.

Life, it seems, is far more than the sum of its physical, explainable, or logical elements.

There is a great amount unseen.

Unexplainable.

Beyond words.

Unseen certainties.

We just know.

CHAPTER 9:
ANOTHER ASSURANCE

I don't recall the exact timing, although I do remember the 'dark' period being about three weeks. Due out of hospital after five to six weeks, there was still a way to go. Around this time, the engineer came in to fix my TV. This was a pretty normal occurrence; people were coming in and out of the room for all sorts of reasons, day and night. But this visitor was special. He was an African and quite chatty. Again, the specifics of the opening conversation are sketchy in my memory, but it involved a book he was reading, and he chatted on as he worked. Somehow it seemed to me that the conversation could be going in an odd direction, as it involved sentences like 'things working out for good... it'll all work out ok, etc etc'. Over the years I have had lots of conversations with people about the power of positive thinking and its viability and limitations, and at this moment, I didn't feel I could cope with any 'deep' conversation; so I simply said something like, 'Derek and I are both Christians', (Derek was there) 'and we believe that God does bring good out of all sorts of situations when we trust Him.' I thought, to be honest, we'd end up with a fixed television and a less chatty engineer – calm restored.

Neither Derek nor I were prepared for what came next. The TV briefly no longer the centre of his attention, our engineer quite literally bounced about, clapping his hands! He was so excited! He, too, was a Christian and as he continued to work on the TV, we all talked together for a few minutes about our faith. Derek prayed with him that day and they shared a prayer daily from then on, with the engineer checking up on us regularly by texts. He even visited us on occasions if he was around when we attended Addenbrookes for subsequent out-patient visits. Apparently, his work covered a large area and he was always pleased to meet with Christians, and felt God called him to be there for us that day. I could wholeheartedly affirm that thought, by telling him how very low I had been feeling, and how poorly, and the way his visit had lifted our spirits. Our contact with him lasted about two years until he began a university course, since which time it has been more infrequent. But what a blessing he was in that season – and no doubt will be to others in the course of his daily work!

Having had this visit and my prayer turning point, I still had two weeks to go before I could leave the hospital. But God, it seems, sometimes has other plans, and within just a few days I was told I could move into the flat on the campus in which Derek was staying. They thought maybe I would recover more speedily if I were out of the hospital environment! Answer to prayer, or what? Words cannot portray how much that change made to me.

I was in the flat for about a week, during which time daily hospital appointments and treatment continued as an outpatient. Derek was by now quite the professional when it came to wheelchair manoeuvres – he knew all the flattest routes and negotiated lifts and kerbs with ease. I could sleep when I needed to, without disturbance. He cooked me little bites as I fancied them; I seem to remember corned beef hash was the first, and what a treat that was. I may not have eaten much, but it was the start of my appetite returning. I had an incredible craving at that time for buttered crumpets – don't ask me why! I might say to Derek 'I think I could eat a crumpet' and one would soon arrive, before the hunger disappeared – day or night. The other thing I recall was a yearning for cheddar biscuits and cheese spread. Not the best of diets, but it served its purpose! That 'as and when' approach to eating continued well after I got home, until such times as my appetite returned fully and I could eat more normally.

Mixed emotions

After that week in the flat, we were able to go home at last, having been in Addenbrookes about five weeks in all. How can I describe my feelings about going home? I am getting accustomed to the fact that there is rarely one single emotion. There was relief, certainly. Having gone through this recent awful period in the hospital in the summer of 2018, I could see that it was coming to an end very soon. There was hope, too. I had survived the second transplant, and there was some future to look forward to. Some anxiety surfaced yet again, because of that sense of security in being surrounded by medical staff; but I knew that if anything untoward occurred someone was just an alarm bell away and my local hospital was just up the road from home.

But amongst all of this, there was the ever-recurring deep sense of gratitude. I had yet more time. How could I spend it well? I believe wholeheartedly that life is a gift from God, none of us has the control over the longevity of our life that we might allow ourselves to believe. So, I saw this next period of my life as a further gift. And for that I was, and continue to be grateful, no matter how long or short it turns out to be.

On arriving home, some lovely friends had filled my garden pots as a welcome home gift (it was early July 2018). Sadly, we arrived home after dark so I would have to wait until the following day to enjoy them. As it turned out, I did not see my flowers for quite a while as my stay at home was short-lived. I had arrived after dark, and by early morning we were back on the road needing to make the increasingly familiar two-hour trip to Addenbrookes hospital, as I was sporting yet another high temperature. Derek had of course, handed in his flat keys the previous day, so he would need yet another place to stay.

Off we went again…

Derek:

We had a lovely couple of years while Jane was in remission, with regular trips down to hospital. Then 'it' came back. And again, I believe God warned me in advance. The same routine was put in place. I had a flat free of charge to live in again, through the same charity. However, the experience was very different. Jane's need for me to be there was much greater, so working during the day was much more difficult and most days I only managed about an hour. When I had worked previously at lunchtime, I slept. Gradually I got further and further behind with work. Some of my hours were picked up by a colleague and my pay dropped. There was nothing I could do other than just keep on visiting and praying. Praying? I had started writing prayers every day and sending them out to the church leadership, then my family, and eventually to about a hundred people all over the UK and several other countries: Germany, USA, Barbados, Nigeria. Those people passed them on to others. I updated those people with news texts and I am sure their prayers held me up and helped Jane too. After five weeks, and a 'false start', we returned home again. We gradually fell into a good routine with me working 5 hours in the morning, walking in the afternoon and/or evening, and Jane slowly improving and picking up the reins at home.

Pat:

Again, the second transplant was scary. All the things that have happened and you have taken them in your stride, very rarely letting anyone know you were feeling down, and I know how much your faith has helped you.

Why?
Anyone who shares in the privilege of raising children will know that from a very young age, the questions "But why?" or "Why not?" are on their lips. And although we may initially applaud their inquisitiveness, is it not too long before we can be rather worn down by the sheer repetition? Does the following sound familiar?
'Please don't go near that iron'
'Why not?'
'Because you could get hurt'
'Why?'
'Because if our fingers touch anything that hot, they get burned'
'Why?'

'Because they are quite sensitive'
'Why?'
'Because God made us that way'
'Why?'
(sighing) 'Just don't touch the iron, ok?'
'Why not?'
… and so, feeling like I could be having this conversation forever, what do I say next?

Yup, you've probably guessed it… something I thought I would never say…

'Because I say so!'

It appears as if we are born curious. And of course, that is no bad thing. Without it, there is little if any progress. When I think about God, and faith-related things, I can get many of my answers from the Bible. But not all of them are easy to see. As with the earlier imagined conversation with my young child, I must ask some questions of myself:

Do I actually want the answer?

Am I simply trying to appear clever?

Am I trying to win an argument?

Show my superiority of knowledge?

Why do I have this need to know and understand everything?

And maybe for me anyway:

How do I respond when I simply haven't the capacity to understand the answer fully, and God says simply 'Because I say so'?

In the previous chapter, you have heard me describe a tortuous three weeks, when I did not understand what God was doing. And if I am perfectly honest, I still don't really. The answers to some 'Why?' questions that we confront God with, are simply beyond us. I heard this described once in a way that made some sense to me. It went something like this. Picture the 'Why?' questions like railway engines, parked in a siding. Every now and again, we fetch them out for a run. In fact, it is good for them to have a run. But it is equally important that we take them back to the siding, to keep the main track free. The questions of 'why?' are important. But they can also become very much a diversion from any progress in our faith, if they become a circular conversation, like that of a parent and a young child.

Parent protects child.
Child doesn't always understand but trusts parent.
Child is safe with parent.
God protects us.
We don't always understand, but trust God.
We are safe with Him.

Maybe that it is why we call it the Christian faith.

CHAPTER 10:
WHAT NEXT? JULY 2018

In Addenbrookes again

From day one, we had been warned that there were likely to be stays in hospital as part of post-transplant recovery – that was considered normal procedure in the 'world of doctor'. However, that had not been my experience the first-time round. During that two-and-a-half-year period, following my first transplant, I had only one in-patient stay due to a chest infection, otherwise it had been outpatient appointments. Throughout that period, I had been aware that I was doing well, but this time round I realised I was maybe starting to experience a more typical response.

So here I was back in a hospital bed - this time in a shared room. A first. I had until now been so cosseted and well cared for, that even the thought of a shared room posed for me a challenge. I am generally, I think, quite a friendly person, but all sorts of fears and worries surfaced.

What would she be like?

Would she be friendly?

Would she chatter on?

What about when I was awake at night – would it cause a problem?

What if I suddenly needed the loo and it was occupied?

Being alone so much in my care had been a real blessing, but clearly it had changed me somehow. And the fear stayed with me quite a while. Being with people, sharing and conversing was something I now needed to work at. Almost like a new skill.

My other concern might seem very trivial to some, but this visit clashed with the 2018 Football World Cup. Unless you are a real football fan, your thought may be 'So what?' Derek, being an avid football fan, may have choices to make. It would have been no problem in a single room – the footie could have been on the TV at any point while he was sitting with me.

What about now?

Would he still visit?

If he did, would he resent missing a match if I were just falling in and out of sleep?

And as you can probably imagine, even if I was awake, my subjects for interesting conversation were rather limited! I don't particularly share his passion for the sport, but as it is a real highlight for him, I certainly did not want to be the reason he was deprived of the enjoyment.

The lady in the next bed was, as it turned out, lovely. We got on well. Her husband also wanted to watch the football, so it became a shared interest. As in so many situations, the worries and fears beforehand were not realised. Why do I find it so hard to remember that, the next time a challenge occurs? I wish I could say I have learned how to, but it constantly becomes a test of my faith. Maybe like all the tests we endured at school, some I passed better than others and some may have warranted the report 'could do better'!

During this stay (fresh from transplant, eating not fully restored) my mainstay diet was bacon rashers (shop-brand only for some reason) and cheesy puffs. I ate them bag by family bag – day and night. It was a source of amusement to my roomie and me!

Summer of 2018

It turned out to be a short stay of around a week. This too passed. When I eventually returned to our home, my garden pots were looking beautiful, and I was able to really appreciate them and the care behind the planting of them. My recuperation followed a very similar pattern to the first-time round, a lot of wheelchair travelling in the beginning with the targets of walking a few more steps, pushing the 'wheels' for support before sitting and having a wheelchair walk.

Not for the first time did I feel fortunate to live so close to the coast, because as it developed into a blisteringly hot summer, Derek was able to take me to the beach in the cool of the evenings. This was lovely. Having spent so much time indoors out of necessity, whether it be at home or in hospital, to be taken along the promenade feeling the breeze against my face was a real joy. Along our local beach, there are benches placed at regular intervals, and I would measure my progress by how many benches I could reach by walking before giving in! Little markers such as these were of considerable importance to me, as they confirmed that I was indeed making progress, albeit in small ways.

Thinking through the considerable support I received, this was particularly special. I know Derek was tired from all the daily tasks, and I would have understood if he simply wanted to collapse in front of the TV in the evenings. But that extra effort did more for me than give me chance to exercise and progress physically; it got me into the fresh air, by the sea, and I cannot overstate how important that little bit of 'normality' was for me. I could smile at strangers and pass the time of day with those taking a rest on the benches. Yes, I was in a wheelchair, but then I was not alone in that; on these evenings I knew that in every other sense, I was a little more like what I remembered of my previous self.

Adapting to a new way of thinking

So many things were now becoming a way of life. Not even a 'while I am poorly' temporary thing, but how things now had to be. Masks at the doctors and hospitals were standard practice – but back then, in 2018, this was mainly limited to places considered high - risk regarding picking up infections, such as hospitals and doctors' surgeries. I was beginning to prepare my trips out differently from those of my pre-Leukaemia days. Each time I left the house I would ask myself such questions as:

Have I Antibac handwipes handy?

Do I need a mask?

Is it safe where I am going? (I made risk assessments all the time)

Have I the energy?

How many people are likely to be there?

Am I up to conversation? And if I wasn't, would I be able to avoid it?

Will there be food there and will it cause a difficulty for me?

My brain was in a whirl in a vain attempt to get some

control of my life.

I was sick and tired – often literally. The summer heat of 2018 could make me quite unwell, so we had a bed downstairs in a cool room for such times. I was fed up with hearing myself say "I'm tired" so goodness knows how others coped with it!

Song:
'Tell your heart to beat again' by Danny Gokey

Is everybody different?
Going through something like this for the second time was indeed different for me. Was that the case for others, too? Perhaps they also thought it was easier the second time round, and I didn't need the same support – after all, I'd done it all before and had come through – and isn't that exactly what had been my own expectation? My initial diagnosis in August 2014 had been a total bolt out of the blue for my friends as well as me. And they would very understandably have been processing their own thoughts along the way; maybe now it was less of a worry? Less of a scare? Maybe more a disappointment or sadness? I don't know of course, and I certainly wouldn't judge. I have thought about my own reaction over the years, having grown up with a chronically ill parent; each bout of illness became in my mind "just another episode" and part of how things were. Normalised, if you like. So, I can recognise how the depth of my response became different with the passing of time all those years ago. Why would I expect anything different from anyone else – it was a totally natural response, but maybe I can learn from my experience and think differently in the future? Is that even possible? I don't know of course, how true it was that others were different, or how much of it was me. All I know is it felt very different this time round. It seemed more "matter of fact" and only those closest to me had much of an insight into what was really going on with me.

Song:
'You're still God' by Philippa Hanna

CHAPTER 11:
COVID MARCH 2020 ONWARDS

I did eventually return to the more usual run of life, although as I've outlined, that was an ever-changing situation for me. I think it would be true to say that by this point I had less of an expectation that this leukaemia might one day be gone- a thing of my past to look back on. It is difficult to say, to be fair, because of course in March 2020 the Covid pandemic had appeared on the scene. I was, along with many, many others incarcerated indoors for twelve weeks by the government! There were special rules for 'people like me'. The general public were encouraged to be careful of their proximity to 'people like me'- the clinically vulnerable.

This was an awful time for most people, each with their own challenges.

Those who needed to work throughout the time and take risks daily on behalf of others- whatever would we have done without delivery drivers and other essential workers?

There were parents cooped up in flats with young children eager to be out, but not having any available, legal outdoor space in which to play.

And home-schooling!

Many lost income, or businesses or dreams.

I can't help but think of those poor people who had elderly relatives in hospitals or care homes and could not visit or support them as they might have been used to.

Those whose respite opportunities were removed and needed to be 24-hour carers for family members with needs of one sort or another.

Left alone to cope as best they could.

One of Derek's relatives, having been diagnosed with inoperable cancer found, along with others, that there was now little opportunity for treatment in hospital and care was left to his wife, supported by her family but only from a distance. And that is not even to mention our debt to the wonderful NHS staff.

The world, it seemed, had turned upside down. For a time, there was much more understanding of the need for infection control for all of us. I thought at the time that I was, in fact, at an advantage in that I had lived for seven years or so very aware of infections, so much of it was second nature to me. And the whole Covid experience maybe encouraged us all in some way to develop a deeper understanding of the challenges other people face in life; and communities started looking out for each other even if it hadn't been our custom before.

Moving on from Covid
The actual period of acute worry was not at all difficult for me because of my history. But coming out of the Covid-mentality was a different story altogether. At best, because of the timing of it all, my emotional recovery rate slowed. At worst it may have set it back. I now had another layer of health worry - this new illness, the long-term effects of which were not yet known. What I experienced of course was the same as many, many others, so I claim no special situation. It will have affected others in different ways. I remember hearing the phrase 'we're all in the same boat' and it being (rightly, in my opinion) challenged with 'No. We may be all in the same storm, but we are in very different boats'. Lots of people wanted to get back to normal as quickly as possible. Perfectly understandable. And enviable. For myself, I had as yet not fully established what a normal life post second transplant even looked like. That had been a work in progress. It was a scary time. There was a lot of comparison going on in many circles, all keen I guess to restore the status quo. Some held back for many different reasons. Some were forging ahead. The non-vaccinated angered many. But this as I see it, is one of the beauties of living in a free country. They had as much right to live freely, as I did to hold back. I can't imagine I was alone in sensing the tension at that time. And I learned early on, that it did no-one any good to play the blame game by being angry with those who chose not to be vaccinated, or who took amazing risks by not following the guidelines set down for the good of society as it was seen then.

Each of us individually was feeling their way and had valid reasons for choosing the way forward that we did. For me it meant returning to a high state of personal protection. When I did start having people to visit in the garden, I would exercise my right and privilege to self-regulate and be selective as to who I was happy to see. It was for me a matter of feeling 'safe'.

Even returning to Church proved challenging. Often to carry out a conversation with me (I continued to wear my face mask in company), people would come closer than I felt comfortable with; and rather than just seeming unfriendly, it was easier to just stay away. Eventually I settled into a pattern of arriving after the service began and leaving in the last hymn. To this day, the risk assessments continue on an event-by-event basis – back then, I was on heightened alert! Back to feeling I needed to justify my position when I chose not to go somewhere. And I know my decisions were sometimes emotional ones. They still are. And surely that is the same for us all to some degree? I feel 'safe' going in shop A, but not Shop B. A friend may be quite content in shop B but not A. Is this not OK?

A short stay in The Paget

Life was becoming interspersed with not only appointments, but the occasional stay in hospital as an in-patient, and during the later stages of the pandemic, I was again back in The Paget. This came about as the result of an infection, although I didn't realise it at the time. I had been feeling generally unwell, and on this occasion, I had passed out in the shower at home, and in so doing managed to break two bones in my big toe. It turned out that my blood pressure was dropping significantly when I stood or moved quickly, and during this in-patient stay I managed to pass out in the bathroom there as well. As a result of that, I was barred from even moving from the bed without being accompanied. This was the one and only time I was not allowed any visitors at all due to the pandemic and risk of further infection.

I was surprised at how well I coped – not feeling well probably helped, as I slept a lot – but I felt for Derek. It must have been very hard for him to rely only on the mobile for communication, especially when his last memory was of rescuing me from the shower and seeing me ushered into the back of an ambulance. For me, it also provided a further insight into how difficult it must have been for people who found themselves in the position of being in hospital with no hope of visitors for a longer period. I was quite used to being there, and of course, the staff were familiar. I also had the privilege of a quiet room. Having had Derek, Jenny and my many other visitors previously I was reminded of how much help that had been. I am certain their presence was a key part of my recovery. But what about the patients who were going through the transplant procedure, or intensive chemotherapy for other conditions, and having to do it alone? It doesn't bear thinking about.

Later when I came out, complete with boot and non-weight-bearing foot, it posed a few extra challenges. Finding a chair I could sit in comfortably was important, enabling my leg to be raised on a stool to help bring down the swelling. Walking with the aid of a frame, I could feasibly have made a cup of tea (balanced on one leg and supported by the frame), but would not be able to carry one. Hopping along, carrying a hot drink like this did not seem to be a viable option! Hence, Derek was back to doing a lot of the work, and we were – just like that – back to wheelchair walks… yet again. But by God's grace, the loan of a very comfortable wheelchair from a friend, and an incredible amount of patience on Derek's part, we got through.

Ongoing support
Although I did find the whole experience very different the second time around in so many ways, friends continued supporting me for the 'long haul'. I found this very humbling and am grateful beyond words. I needed to continue to lean on God and friends. I cannot begin to explain how the Life Group I am part of supported me through this time and I will always be grateful for that.

Meeting online regularly.

Waiting patiently for me to be ready to return to face-to-face communication.

For some time they met in person, and I joined them 'on the mantelpiece' on someone's phone!

How kind they were to help me feel as comfortable and safe as I could when I did return. Interestingly, I am sure some of them would consider that I was maybe being a bit over the top… or that they would have done things differently… and that is ok. They *never* imparted that to me. They simply accepted that was where I was at and went with it for my well-being.

Dear Lord, may I honour others in this way when they and I differ in our approach to any given situation.

My friend, An (no, not a typo, that is her name!), is also my prayer partner, and she was an amazing support, before, during and after the Covid episode. I found the transition out of pandemic mode extremely challenging. I often get a picture in my mind as I pray which helps me to understand and describe how I am feeling, and on this occasion I told her that it felt like I was in a "trench" stuck on a dark route which I didn't know, and didn't like. Above me and around were people free from the trench, seemingly having a wonderful life denied to me. When I tried to venture out and join them, finding it to be scary and dangerous, I found I was no more in control there anyway. As we prayed together I "saw" in my mind's eye as it were, that I was being lifted higher, but supported underfoot, so that I was part of everything alongside others, feeling freer. And I began to recognise my "trench" as a picture of a God-given safe place to stay close to; I did not need to be confined by it. It was lighter, and I had a better view, so it was not anywhere near as scary. My friend saw her part as being in her own personal "trench" alongside mine, following the route her life was taking, and it would stay that way until such times as our trenches diverged.

This helped me often over the subsequent months, as she would often remind me on bad days to get back to my 'trench' and by so doing, stay close to or in the safety of where I needed to be. My life was going a particular route, not of my choosing, but God knew what was best for me, as for everyone, and was showing me that it could be after all a good place, and I continued to be safe with Him. I now see all these things as a part of my moving forward in ways I could handle, but always progressing. She and my life group were often the first, after my family, to know of any significant changes in my circumstances, so they were able to pray for me while I had time to process my thoughts before telling the 'rest of the world' as it were.

Stepping down
What else can I say about these four years after the second transplant? In many ways, it was very simply a case of 'more of the same' – or as my friend Pat would say 'same old, same old'! It was proving to be a much tougher road to physical recovery, but the principles remained the same.

Avoid infections.
Take care.
Try new situations.
Get involved where I could.
Learn what to avoid.
Constantly dealing with the emotional ups and downs of varying intensities.
Try to make each day count.
Appreciate the preciousness of time and not waste it.

It is, I suppose, not wise for any of us to take time for granted. To this end, we did make a change. After the first transplant, friends had helped with the cleaning, until I could pick it up again. The second time round, we made the decision to pay for a cleaner for a short period of time, to help us out. This was quite difficult for me; it felt rather like a cop-out, a defeat, almost. But I must admit I was very glad of it. When I had recovered sufficiently to consider doing the cleaning again, it began a discussion between Derek and me. My point was that for the most part I was now quite capable of cleaning the house; I could do it bit by bit, rather than the previous weekly blitz! I couldn't justify the expense. Or the luxury.

He reminded me of my 'traffic lights' system.
Was it a red, green or amber activity?
Did it take a lot of energy?
What about if I had a 'low battery' day when the housework needed to be done, because we had run out of laundry,

everything was in the ironing basket, or it proved to be a choice between having a cooked meal or a clean house?

Was it a good use of my limited energy?

He was right, of course. Technically, I was able to do housework, but it most definitely would be a question of weighing up energy levels. Did I really want to spend that precious limited energy on housework at the expense of having the opportunity to paint, visit a friend, or anything else I found uplifting?

So, the decision was eventually made that we would continue to have our house cleaned, and I could do as little or much as I chose to in between these visits. When circumstances change, it appears it helps if we adapt to them. It's a decision I've never regretted.

Unhealthy obsession

One thing I recall quite clearly was a rather disturbed phase I went through. You will likely be aware by now, that by nature I am a 'do-er'. I also have a thing about lists, which is often not to my advantage! Derek and I had become aware that we needed to think through practicalities regarding what I was currently doing toward the home living that would need to be continued in my absence, whether it be due to long term deterioration of health, or death. So, I set about preparing for any eventuality. Over 40 years or so, there were systems in place only known to me. Things Derek rarely, if ever, had needed to think of.

Where is the bedlinen kept?

Did he know that I had marked each corner of a fitted sheet with K or D, so that which ones fitted any given bed was clear to anyone?

Did he know they were kept in different places for ease?

Did he know the tea towels and hand towels needed to be changed regularly?

Would he think about cleaning through the dishwasher/washer from time to time?

You get the idea.

There is a lot that goes on behind the scenes in a home, which seems to work 'by magic'!

They are just simply - done!

And in fairness, it works both ways; I depend heavily on Derek for other practical jobs around the place.

All of this of course, is not a bad idea at all for any of us really.

Like making a will.

Sharing vital passwords for bank details.

There are so many things that just one partner in a relationship takes primary responsibility for.

Unfortunately, I got into the mentality of, 'I must have everything always up to date, so that Derek will be set up.

What if I needed to go into hospital tonight?

There must not be a backlog of washing.

The ironing basket needs to be empty.

The food cupboards must be stocked.

The next meal must be planned.

The bedlinen must be washed immediately when the bed is changed…'

I realise now that it became an unhealthily huge thing for me.

A totally unnecessary burden for me to carry.

And as the saying goes, 'a woman's work is never done', these tasks never had an endpoint. Consequently, while I was thinking like this, nothing else got done.

There was little free time.

And I was constantly tired.

Not exactly life to the full!

Thankfully, after a few weeks, I recognised it for what it was. But it was one of the many learning curves I experienced during this period, and a trap I still occasionally fall into from time to time even today.

All in all, my physical recovery time after the second transplant lasted around four years. The next change came about in March 2022 and more about it in the next chapter.

Queues

According to Reddit.com there is a Dutch joke about the British love of queueing, and it is this:

"A Brit walked down the street and sees two queues. He

gets behind one of them, and asks the woman in front of him: 'What is this queue for?'"

George Mikes, a Hungarian-British journalist and humourist, makes the following observation:

"An Englishman, even if he is alone, forms an orderly queue of one."

I am not a well-travelled person, so I cannot comment on the difference between our perceived culture and that of others, but this queuing trait does seem to be quite often a source of amusement for others. I remember, as a child, visiting the bank or post office with my Mum. In those days, each counter had a separate queuing line, and we would join one of the queues moving toward a certain counter assistant, while watching the other queues carefully to see if it was shortening more quickly than ours. Was it worth switching lanes to get to the front more quickly? Should we just take our chances and stay put? And oh, the frustration when we chose to switch queues, and found ourselves to be subsequently 'stuck' behind a person with a time-consuming transaction, while watching the queue we had left moving steadily on!

On some occasions we would hear an exclamation of,

'Hey! You just took my place… I was in front of you'

Or a more covert muttering of,

'Did you see that? That woman over there just pushed in front of me'.

Very, very occasionally this would escalate into a jostling for front position to which we might hear the cashier's voice above it all "Stand in line please; I can only deal with one person at a time". So logical. So true. There really was no point in four people getting to the front of the queue, all talking at the same time, because at the end of the day, we had to be served individually anyway.

My point? I have concluded in recent years that, although I was born in England, my emotions are possibly not British! They do not queue. They jostle, they tumble over each other and vie for my attention. So often it seems we are, during our life, juggling several emotions simultaneously. Is it possible to feel thankful and grateful at the same time as feeling frustrated or disappointed? How can it be that I can feel contented and at peace at one level, whilst simultaneously experiencing anger or a yearning for an earlier time? When I think of it considering the "queuing" picture, it begins to make some sense. All of those feelings are vying for my attention; one is paramount - at the front of the queue making its voice heard - while another fights for its place.

"Stand in line please; I can only deal with one emotion at a time."

I was intrigued by one of Jenny's comments (at the end of chapter 3) which referred to "one of many times where my emotions and my logic didn't function well together" I can empathise with this. Because while all this emotional jostling is going on, with all its ensuing turmoil, the voice of logic pipes up; 'This isn't helping. You're doing no good here'. And that is logical. That is true.

And then there are the questions about where God is in it all… When I talk it out with God (praying) I find the very process helps me to put it all in order (queueing in line) from which point I can start to deal with each emotion one at a time.

In a more orderly fashion.

Is this emotion helpful?

Do I know why it is so strong in me?

Is it bringing me more in line with what I know of God's word? (e.g. Does the Bible encourage me to be angry? If I am, is it in line with Gods anger? Is there something I could do about it, so that my anger is abated? Or am I simply angry because I haven't got my own way?)

I find the more negative emotions tend to shout the loudest, but when they are analysed in this way, they can become subdued; and the more peaceful ones tend to be quietly and patiently waiting in line, and particularly resilient.

Ready to step forward and take their place.

What a gift this is.

CHAPTER 12:
HERE WE GO AGAIN: MARCH 2022

Although aware that most infections come from within our own body and are therefore for the most part unavoidable, for years I had aimed to avoid contracting any infections from others. Around March 2022, things took a turn for the worse; I felt generally unwell – I couldn't say I was ill, I just didn't feel 'right' – but I did have a high temperature and that was, as always, a gateway to being admitted on the ward. My infection markers, which they like ideally to be in single figures, were over 200. They started talking about me having a viral infection. I knew it was bad as I was, by then, coughing up blood, so was very relieved to be told it wasn't a chest infection. If ever that became the case, there was always a fear of it developing into pneumonia which I would have found worrying, to say the least. So what was it? I had caught a cold. The common cold!

I remember laughing with my doctor when he started talking about Rhinovirus, and I said, 'So basically you are telling me I have a cold? I can't wait to tell my friends. Most people when they get a cold, just get on with it – not me!' In my mind continuing with, 'I get 7 days in bed, 3 meals a day and am on intravenous antibiotics.' It can be quite comical when you think of it that way, and Derek and I both find it helpful to laugh at the situation when we can – but of course, they kept saying this is a "very serious" infection. Maybe they thought I wasn't taking it seriously, but I knew the score. This was simply a reminder of the reality I lived. I lived a carefully managed life and had managed to avoid the common ailments for a long time, but it is not possible to avoid them all, if you are to have any life at all.

At the end of the week, blood counts still low, I was given a blood transfusion. That certainly felt like a step backwards, as I hadn't needed one of those since the latest transplant some four years ago. When I mentioned this, I was told that it was just a precaution… it would give me a boost for when I went home. We would have to wait and see but they would schedule a bone marrow test to see where we were at. They are always so careful and kind about how they phrase things to us patients, but of course, after a lot of practice at 'hospital speak' I could read between the lines. So, yet again, I knew what was coming. The inevitable result? The leukaemia was taking hold again. This was confirmed on a follow up appointment by a young doctor who on this occasion seemed visibly saddened at having to tell me such news. He was so apologetic. What an awful part of their job such appointments must be for the consultants. I told him much the same as I've told doctors before and since. That I was extremely grateful for everything they had done for me to get me this far, and I had enjoyed so much time with my grandchildren that I had not anticipated. And I meant every word. And of course, it was not the shock for me that maybe he had assumed, thanks to my previous experience of relapse.

So, what now?

I had it explained to me again, as I had so many years back, that I would be put on an outpatient cycle of chemo injections. Three injections a day, on this occasion, for five days every five weeks. Well, it was better than seven! As is always the case for me, knowing I had a pattern to my life made things so much better. It gave me more of a sense of control. I now pictured my life ahead in these sections:

Week 1: Chemo daily
Week 2: 'Low blood' week. Less energy maybe
Week 3: Recovery and enjoy life a bit. See friends. Maybe go away to family.
Week 4: Enjoy life. See friends. Maybe go away
Week 5: More of the same including a consultant appointment in readiness for the following weeks treatment. Get any other appointments done, while at my strongest, e.g. dentist, hygienist, optician, etc.

Yes, I could handle that! I say 'I' rather than 'we' simply because Derek naturally has very much more of a 'deal with it as it comes' mentality than I naturally manage. We could plan stays away and have a vague idea about how I would be on any given day.

What a joke!

When will I learn?

Will I ever learn that I am not in control?

None of us really are, are we?

Life for us all is an ever-changing beast.

From feast to famine; from joy to sorrow; from hope to despair; and everything in between. And it can, as it did with me, change in a flash.

How thankful I am that God is constant through it all.

The steadying hand.

The anchor.

With this in mind, I focussed on the pattern of life and was ready to proceed. As if to underline and emphasise the point, two months into my new chemo cycle, my bloods chose not to recover. At a face-to-face appointment on a follow-up visit to Addenbrookes, I was presented with my results in the usual fashion. The conclusion of that meeting was that the chemotherapy itself was doing me more harm than good, so they proposed that they stopped what they call 'active treatment' of the disease and were considering other options. Basically, they would stop trying to conquer the leukaemia and focus on improving my quality of life while managing (what I assumed would be) my inevitable decline. I realise in retrospect, that again Derek and I were essentially calm. I remember us walking down the corridor from the consultation room that day talking in the same 'matter of fact' way as if we were discussing the weather, or what we were going to have for dinner.

A new drug had been mentioned as an option, but it was not usually prescribed on the NHS - was it something we could financially consider? I cannot remember the exact figure – I might not even have heard it – it might not have been specified, but it was not at all in our thinking to go down that route. I think our faces/immediate reaction (or was it the stifled laughter at the thought?) was enough to stop that line of enquiry! There might be a trial going - he wasn't aware of one, but he could look into it – was that something I might be interested in? The answer was in principle, yes, I'd been on trials already, but I'd naturally need to know details before I decided.

The other option was supportive care. Not palliative, he said, that's different. Supportive care means in essence that they would monitor me regularly, and treat infections as and when they occurred. Almost simultaneously I seem to remember, we were all following the same train of thought. I wonder what your next question would have been? I started with words along the lines of 'I don't suppose you can give me any idea…' and he finished for me. No, he couldn't say how long. I could remain healthy for quite a while, or I could get an infection the following week that they couldn't beat with antibiotics… He remained, as do most consultants I have seen, very kind, very honest and almost apologetic. This was of course nothing new. In a sense, it has been like that since day one at some level or another. It certainly had become my way of life, infection-avoidance, so I could honestly say on behalf of us both, that we understood. And we really did. I said that we were grateful for all they had done so far, and were continuing to do, and we would see where this took us.

So, as we walked down that corridor, there was an outside chance of a trial, which we may or may not have considered depending on what was involved, but it appeared that the option we needed to get our heads around in the absence of an alternative active treatment, was the final one.

Supportive care.

I remember saying to Derek that we needed to be prepared to be thinking weeks rather than months, as we know this leukaemia can be aggressive when it takes hold. With no chemo to hold it back, and very low blood counts, I would probably find it difficult to fight any infection. He reminded me, as he often does as such turning points, "We're in this together" and we would face it that way. We looked to God again for peace and security, and yes, hope. For now, and the ultimate future. Yes, we could – and would – face it together.

What's going on?

This all happened at the end of July 2022. The following week, I resumed the regular blood tests at the James Paget, which were now mainly with a view to monitoring my situation. Derek and I have always agreed along with our 'children' that they would be informed at every stage, no matter how difficult. To this end, we had already had conversations with each of them regarding the news we had received and the subsequent changes. They, too, needed time to process the information.

Chemo had been stopped.

Medication had been stopped.

At my second monitoring visit (very soon after the visit where I was told they were stopping the active treatment – I think within seven days), I had blood tests taken as usual at the James Paget, and I was called through into a separate room to discuss the results with my specialist nurse. This was common practice. What came next though, broke from the expected. I'll not forget in a hurry the conversation as we walked along the corridor.

'I've got your results. I've checked them, because I needed to know I'd got the right results…. In fact, I've checked them twice.'

Whatever was coming?

As we sat down in the room, she told me… my bloods had recovered.

Recovered?

'I know, I didn't believe it at first either, that's why I made sure to check them. Yes, they have recovered. They are back in the normal range'.

Normal?

'Yes'.

What was going on? What would you think at this point?

Was this coincidence? Had I been misinformed?

Had I misunderstood?

But no, I have noted my results with interest all through so that I, along with the doctors, could see the prevailing trend at any given time. I am not good with shocks, and as if you haven't gathered it by now, I like to have an idea what is coming along!

As I looked back at my recent recorded results, they were indeed at one point extremely low. My immunity capability had registered at 0.04. Now, I haven't a clue what that means scientifically, but even I could see that was virtually non-existent! A reading of 4 and above is OK. 2 or under, low-ish. Under 1, getting a little concerned. Under 0.5 neutropaenic (lots of dietary and health limitations at this point). And I was registering at 0.04. As I have said, I can often see the comical side of these things and I remember having said to this same nurse then, 'so basically, you're saying I haven't got any immunity to speak of… I haven't got any infection-fighting-capability to all intents and purposes…? Well, I will make it my aim to get into minus numbers and set a record low'! Joking aside, this was happening.

Now, it all seemed to have turned around by itself, and I had blood results in the normal parameters. And by the August of 2022, medication had been reinstated and I was put back onto the chemo cycle once more. We did question why they were recommencing the chemo treatment, as it seemed to me that the recovery had taken place after the chemo had been stopped. Their view was that the chemo had done the job, but my blood had just been slow to pick up. Basically, we agreed, as we had previously decided we would go with the doctors' recommendations even if we didn't understand. It does however fascinate me that, in over a year of regular chemo since this event, my bloods have never had a problem recovering in the allotted time at all. Intriguing.

Life goes on around me
As an 'aside' to all this going on, our daughter had had an accident, just the previous month, in early June 2022. It's interesting to me, that in times of illness, which sometimes can overtake all your mental and emotional energy, life goes on around you. All the ups and downs continue, and we still must be able to deal with them. Nothing stands alone. One life affects another. Our daughter had a simple trip on her landing at home, just walking from one room to another, which resulted in serious breaks in her leg. Tibia, fibula, ankle and toe. We had a phone call on June 9th (in my 'extremely low'

blood count period) from a daughter very much in agony, alone in the house except for her 3-year-old daughter looking on. We tried to comfort her on the phone as best we could while she waited for her husband to get home from work to be with her. But there was so little else we could do except pray and wait. And thank God she had her phone in her pocket at that moment.

It wasn't the first time we had felt helpless. This had happened previously during the Covid lockdown of 2020 when our grandson was born. A lockdown baby. We couldn't visit. Couldn't help. Even without the lockdown restrictions, it would have been difficult for me to consider myself any sort of support to anyone. I could quite easily have become more of a burden than a help. This has been one of the hardest things to deal with. As a mum, I wanted very much to be there for my children and grandchildren as my mum had been for me throughout my years of parenting. Maternal feelings such as these do not stop just because one is ill. It's simply another thing to which we must adjust. Derek did make a trip to Derby at the first possible opportunity, visiting Jenny on behalf of both of us and staying a couple of nights to help support Sam and Katie at home. It was clear to us both that it was not sensible for me to go with my bloods being as low as they were, and I wouldn't be much of a support anyway. Maybe more of a worry. This was a difficult decision. Particularly for Derek, I imagine, because as much as he wanted to see Jenny, he was worried about leaving me. The latter concern was settled by having friends 'on call' for this period, with access to our house key, in case of emergency. My tendency to feel unwell and pass out was at the time a matter of particular concern, but with 'babysitters' in place, we were both settled.

So, here we were with our daughter in hospital, confined to a bed with her leg in a frame to try to support her fractured bones. She was to have a bone re-set and two surgeries under general anaesthetic during her three-week stay. I told my consultant and nurse at my appointment about the situation, being acutely aware of the state of my bloods, but desperate to find a way to see her, if only the once. I am always aware of what they do consistently on my behalf, and I never take them for granted. The least I can do is live by the rules. It may seem that I was asking permission, and maybe I was in a way, but I did want them to say it was ok to go. Was there any way I could do a visit? I really wanted to see her, bearing in mind that at this point, she had been told the severity of the 4 breaks. There had it seemed, also been nerve damage which was causing the extreme pain and she had been warned of the probability that she might not walk unaided in the future and could possibly need a wheelchair. What mother wouldn't want to be there?

They understood totally. If I went straight there on an evening visit - from car to ward - wearing a more protective mask - stayed for the visiting time - went straight back to the car, that should be ok. This conversation took place on a Thursday, the weekend would be the best time to go, and there was no time to even get the necessary mask, as I could see. But I had their blessing in principle. The following day I had my scheduled appointment at Addenbrookes, and I relayed the situation to them – and we were in practical terms halfway to Derby at this very moment. They agreed; we should go. My consultant promptly went to fetch me a couple of masks – 'these are the ones the nurses wear whilst dealing with Covid'. She warned me that they weren't comfortable, but they would be the most protective. So off we went continuing our 8-hour round trip to my daughter's hospital in Derby. We had arranged with Jen's husband that there would be no other visitors that evening so that we could make the most of this small window of opportunity. We were of course the last people Jenny expected to see walk round the corner and just to see her face made the trip worthwhile. There were a few tears, I held her hand (she antibacced first!) and what a lovely gift that couple of hours was.

By the way, the consultant had not been exaggerating about how uncomfortable the masks were! How the nurses and doctors coped with it day in day out was a wonder to me. And their sacrifices on our behalf were recognised and applauded by me even more than they had been previously.

Now, a few weeks later, still on the 5-weekly chemo schedule, month by month, I was being told my blood levels were good. At all points.

So, I asked one day 'Does this mean I am normal?'

'Yes'.

'So, I don't need to mask up all the time?'

'Well, it's a good idea to mask up to keep on the safe side'.

'So, I can live more normally (whatever that is) and just continue to wear a mask?'

'Mmmmm. It's probably best to avoid over-crowded places. Or hot places. Meet outside when you can, and if you have to be indoors, make sure it is a well-ventilated area'.

'So, not exactly normal then?'

It is such a strange position to be in. When I was ill, even when I was not in hospital, I knew where I was, what I could do, what I could not do. It had been pretty obvious. Now, I was 'well' in terms of the hospital, the treatment was working; my results were good; but negotiating life on the outside is not as easy as it may seem to the on-looker. Covid didn't help. The fact that I looked so well didn't help. This is not a complaint. I was, and still am, very grateful to even be in such a position, but it is not always straightforward.

Song:
'Truth I'm standing on' by Leanna Crawford

On one occasion I commented that I was aware it was possible for an acute leukaemia to develop into a chronic form of the illness. My leukaemia had now relapsed twice since the initial diagnosis, were they still treating this as 'acute' (i.e. potentially curable, could be over one day) or 'chronic' (recurring)? The answer was unexpected. Yes, it is still an acute disease, but we are needing to treat it as chronic. It appeared as if this was not going the way that was to be expected perhaps? I reminded the nurse about the time I was taken off chemo and medication and then my bloods recovered. Yes, she remembered.

Where was God in all this? Was that week with no active treatment which resulted in blood recovery His way of saying 'I've got this – it's not only the chemo that is making you well' or was it just one of those things that happened? I genuinely don't know. I believe that God made us, and our bodies are amazing. They have inbuilt healing qualities – in simple terms, just think of a cut, if kept clean, the skin left to itself will heal over. Think of the millions of cells in different parts of our bodies, all with their unique functions. What information a blood test gives us. Think of the knowledge the doctors have, to work alongside and make things better and often easier for us. Where does that come from, if not God? I have long believed that God and doctors bring healing in conjunction with each other. They are not in competition in any way.

At one point when I was praying, I said, "Lord, if You are choosing to heal me so that I have a leukaemia-free life ahead, then the chemo will have to stop with the doctors' agreement. I cannot make that call. I could be so wrong." I even added "To be honest, if You wrote it in the sky with skywriting, I still couldn't be certain." To add to my confusion, on June 4th this very year 2023, at Church there were, as part of the service, about fifteen unmarked envelopes scattered around the building for the congregation to find. I randomly picked one. Inside was a scripture verse as a prompt for prayer for the recipient.

When I opened mine, this was what was inside:

"Jesus turned and saw her. 'Take heart, daughter' He said, 'Your faith has healed you'. And the woman was healed at that moment." (Matthew 9 v 22 NIV)

What was I to make of this? Coincidence? I genuinely don't know. All throughout, we have hoped and prayed for the best, whilst preparing for the worst. So I couldn't, and can't, allow myself to be hopeful only to be let down by being wrong. I try to focus on the journey and God's part in it, rather than its conclusion. And of that I can be certain.

Is this doubt?
Lack of faith?
Is it a total cop-out?
Again, I don't know.

Maybe it's a mixture of all three.

Derek and I have always followed the doctors' lead and we trust them to do their best.

They always have. So, we both concluded that we will leave it to them.

Jenny:

In early 2022, I was at the church toddler group with my daughter, and a friend (who reminds me a lot of a cross between my Mum and my Nan) was asking how my mum was doing and even though I thought I was okay that day (nothing particular had happened as far as I remember) I just suddenly started sobbing and the overwhelming thing that came out that day was "I still need her…"

If I'm not sure how to get a stain out of a t-shirt, or something is bothering me and I don't know why, or Katie has a temperature and I'm not sure how long to leave it, when we're making a big decision and I need to run it past someone or I just can't remember how to make custard, or just ANYTHING really – it's still Mum I call. I don't have that sense that "I've got this" with life, and I still have so much to learn from her – not just the practical day-to-day things, but the big life things – how to raise a teenager, how to handle sibling squabbles, how to cope when things suddenly change course. And it's not just the knowledge and wisdom that she has, but the sense of being really really known. Nobody knows me the way that Mum and Dad do. There are lots of people who have known me for many many years, some I've got to know well in the last 10-15 years, but they don't know the things that shaped me over the years or what I was like as a seven-year-old. And there are many other people who knew me well as a child/teen/young adult who don't really know me now – how I've changed, grown, matured. Mum and Dad know all versions of me over every season and the thought of losing those people is really scary.

And on this day at toddler group, I had this terror

suddenly overwhelm me that Mum has taught me so much over the years and said so many words. What about all the times I wasn't paying full attention because I was half-concentrating on dishing up dinner? Or I've just plain forgotten? Or I wrote it off because I didn't agree at the time? And I thought about the times that she'd tell me a story and I know I've heard it before but it's just one of many many things we've talked about over the years and it just hasn't stuck in my memory and I needed reminding. And I just sobbed and sobbed on my friend, because I knew that I was never going to "get there" when it came to not needing Mum and one day, even if it was a long day in the future, I was going to not be able to ask her any more questions.

I've got a bit more used to the ups and downs in the day-to-day than I was in the early days, but that's still one feeling that is as intense as it was back in August 2014. And although, at time of writing, we've had 9 extra years, it just never feels like it could be enough.

I still have regular moments like this, that vary in size and impact, but that day was significant for me, because it did help me to put into perspective that whether we had a few more months or 30 more years, it was never going to be enough for me, and so the main thing was just to appreciate and value it every day extra we do get. And to be thankful to God for every additional day He grants. And I really am.

Processes

As I have reflected on the many stages of the last ten years, it is becoming increasingly apparent to me that there are few fundamental aspects of life which have an endpoint, or maybe I should say a defined endpoint. There are of course some practical examples such as a starting day at school or work, and leaving school, changing jobs, or retiring. Each can usually be linked to a particular date in time. Writing a shopping list, going shopping, putting said shopping into appropriate cupboards… job done. Over.

But when it comes to the more 'internal' side of life, is it so clearly defined? We are constantly growing, changing, developing, learning. Our relationships often fluctuate between an intense closeness to each other – during a time of grief, for example – and the more mundane. During my many years of doing the school 'drop-off' each morning, I would see certain people on an almost daily basis, and some friendships would develop – but then, due to a change of class/school, it would be 'all change'. But I had not consciously stopped the relationship. Neither had my previous friends (I hope!) In fact, since retiring, some friendships have been rekindled even more strongly.

When I read Jenny's reflection, it came home to me quite strongly that our journeying through leukaemia is a process which had a somewhat sudden beginning but is unlikely to have a defined end – not only for myself, but for my family. All our individual experiences will have been assimilated into our being, continuing to shape our character. It is my understanding that no experience is ever forgotten. It may go into our subconscious, but it is still there. This is the way we have been designed. We are a 'work in progress'. The process continues. When I consider my family particularly, I am incredibly saddened to think that their processing of what I have come to think of as the 'leukaemia situation' will continue, as does mine. They too will have their ups and downs, and sometimes as Jenny recognises, not for any particular external reason. Will there ever be an endpoint to this? I don't know.

When I was preparing to leave school in the mid 1970's, I experienced the beginnings of career advice. Long before the days of Apps or internet sites where one can find the ideal job, we were 'helped' to make our career decisions. One valid question regarding this is I think, "Do you prefer to be a smaller part of a big project, or take a smaller task from the start and see it through to completion?" Although I do like to enjoy the process, I do rather need to have defined endpoints. I was fortunate in my job as a piano teacher; although the process of learning an instrument never actually stops, there are well-defined markers or stages which are quantifiable, whether that was in the form of an examination and subsequent certificate, or simply the mastery of a piece or completion of a book.

What are the end-points I see (or engineer) in my situation? Because I'm pretty sure I do.

A course of tablets comes to an end. Tick.

I stay well all through a holiday. Tick.

I prepare and lead a life group meeting. Tick.

When I think of the overall picture of my life, it is too overwhelming. Rather like the overwhelming reaction Jenny described when she was with her friend.

But the process is underway.

It cannot be stopped by me, or anyone else.

I could one day be the recipient of the words that we hear tearfully spoken on the 'Let's Beat Cancer' TV adverts; "It's gone!"

But I doubt it somehow.

How would we know?

What is my defined endpoint?

So, I must learn to live with the process, as best I can, in my bite-size manageable pieces. As Jesus himself said,

"So don't worry about tomorrow, for tomorrow will bring its own worries. Today's trouble is enough for today"

Matthew 6:34 (NLT)

If only it were so simple.

CHAPTER 13:
WHAT NOW? 2023

As I am writing this now, August 2023, I am sixteen days away from the 9th anniversary of my diagnosis. There have been so many turning points, that I can sometimes feel as if I am spinning. Many dates are forever etched on my brain. – dates and events I will never forget. Events I remember but with no dates attached. These have shaped me, sometimes for the better, I think, and sometimes most certainly not. I have had my faith both tested and affirmed. I have felt fear in ways I didn't before. Where previously I had a clear ministry purpose – raising children – heading up children's work at Church – more latterly, working with the 'Young at Heart' – now I flounder more. I have for many years known that my salvation does not depend on what I do (Thank God!) – and I still believe this to be true. But have I in some underhand way been duped into living that way? So many of these purposes are not applicable anymore, how do I find a new one?

On one occasion I had an interesting conversation with An as we prayed together (one of many conversations actually). For some years I had been learning German and during Covid my lessons needed to stop. Later, when restrictions had been lifted and I was out and about a bit more, my logic told me that it was a waste of time and money now to pick it up again. After all, what's the point of such an investment in the future? My reason for learning had been that I could at least carry out some basic conversation with the German side of my family. Was I likely to ever see them again anyway? What was the point? This is when my friend asked me "Do you enjoy it?" The answer to that was an unequivocal Yes. My German lessons had been a highlight of my month. That was her challenge to me. What was wrong with simply doing something that I liked? Just for pleasure? And it was a challenge for me. As I considered my 'previous life', how manic it had been in many ways. How little time I had found to spend simply with friends. How little time I had to pursue the hobbies and desires that God had given me. I love so many things… why would God give anyone a desire to paint/act/cook/do sport or music, or indeed any hobby, and then prohibit them enjoying such pursuits by ensuring they were constantly otherwise busy? Why had it been so difficult to find time for a proper Sabbath Rest?

On the other hand, I was sure that God had/has a purpose for me for the rest of my life here, as He does for all of us. I did not want to go from everything to nothing. I have been asked, 'How do I live with the uncertainty?' That's really interesting to me, as I have really struggled with this very question in practical terms. But all of us live with a similar uncertainty in the sense that we none of us know what will happen in our life in the future. Maybe I had, before my diagnosis, been simply going through life 'blissfully unaware', under the assumption that I would live until old age as had my mum and nan. The knowledge of my medical condition, however, has subsequently encouraged me to think about life differently.

I do still have days like Jenny described when the whole situation is totally overwhelming, as if I am back to square one, as it were, and completely lost. I had an incident only recently in fact, when I attempted to do a 'new' thing; to try to mix in a different social setting; the upshot of which was the beginnings of a panic attack and I needed to escape. I was not, it appears, ready for that particular step forward as yet. But I am learning to draw on the many things I have experienced over these years, the many things I have learned about myself, about God, and about life generally. And as in the words of an old song by Jerome Kern "I pick myself up, dust myself off and start all over again'!

Whilst I am negotiating the ups and downs of this roller-coaster ride I seem to be on, the world keeps turning. For the vast majority it is simply just another day. It is like I am in the same world as I always was, but have changed onto a different track, while people around me remain how they were. Some inevitably have had their own roller-coaster nightmare – not having the same outcome as myself. How do I come to terms with hearing the news of a young child dying of cancer? Or a parent of young children, with a very similar diagnosis to me, whose body was not able to beat the infections long enough to be able to have the gift of a transplant?

I'm not sure that I have, or ever will.

Medically I continue to do well, although recently I have had 2 bone marrow tests which have proved inconclusive – leaving us unsure of the prevalence or even the presence of leukaemia in my body. When I questioned this, the response I received was that it looked as if my bone marrow was "underactive." Maybe five weeks wasn't long enough for the marrow to recover between treatments? It might be a good idea to extend the length of time between the chemotherapy weeks? The other way of looking at it was, as things seem to be on an even keel, 'if it ain't broke, don't try to fix it'. And that's the option that has been chosen. And as I say this, it is good to remember that all decisions are made after much discussion between the doctors and myself. I have been thankfully guided by their experience and expertise, but never bulldozed into anything I was not comfortable with.

So, I continue the 5-weekly cycle. A question remains. If the bone marrow is underactive, how come the bloods are good – bearing in mind the bone marrow is instrumental in producing the blood? We all agree, I think, that it is strange. So, we leave it at that. I continue with the challenge of living day to day and not making long term plans with any expectancy. I try to hold everything lightly…. when I can!

Only the other day, after my usual week of chemotherapy, I had blood tests done, as per normal, and they had not dropped at all… in fact one element had risen! Curious…

Christmases and New Year celebrations with the family remain very special, but I cannot avoid that thought; that it could be my last. Don't get me wrong, this is not morbid. I do not go through the whole time thinking this, but I would be lying if I said it didn't cross my mind.

Birthdays are similar, but more weighted toward the remembrance that I have had nine more birthdays than I might have done (in fact since starting to write this down, I have had my tenth)

I am very aware that I have lost confidence in a great deal. Doing my own shopping. Driving myself to places outside the close locality. Making decisions. For 35 years I had run a home successfully and raised three children. I was not an incapable woman. But the latter years have put a big question mark in so many areas of my life.

Can I?
Should I?
Is it safe?
Am I well enough?
Is it too much?
Can I/Should I do it alone?
And there are more!

Again, please don't get me wrong - I am not, as it may sound, in a constant state of terror. But these are a regular part of my thought processes. I am consciously working on this side of things and aiming to do more to build up my confidence and independence. I am driving out of the village alone more often, going to different cafes or restaurants, and taking up more of my share of the day to day 'popping up the shop because we've run out of something'. Although I consciously try not to go somewhere in the pouring rain, thereby needing to stay in wet clothes for a while, I am not averse to rain per se. Such a simple thing, which prior to 2014 I would have thought little if anything about; but when that fear of becoming ill takes a hold, it's a scary place to be.

I am beginning in many ways to feel much more like the 'me' I remember; although it feels as if some things may never be totally restored. But when I am walking out in the rain or blustery wind, I still try to remember to say a quick thank you to God, as I recall the long days in the hospital looking out of the window and wishing I just could be out there, whatever the weather! At these points I am more aware of how far I have come and that brings me joy. Not only for my sake, of course, but for Derek who has carried the brunt of things for a long time.

Counselling of a different kind
At one point in this final stage of 'holding chemo' as I've come to think of it, I was feeling particularly low and did have some counselling; and I would most definitely recommend this sort of support for anyone struggling as a patient or carer. It was really helpful. There was a sense in which I felt freed up to speak probably even more honestly with a professional who I didn't know at all. The anonymity of it was liberating. I was fortunate enough to have 5 sessions with two different lady counsellors. Each highlighted different aspects for me; mostly clarification and verification of what I was finding out about myself and my situation. Some were more surprising.

I think the trauma of the initial event, the sudden change of direction for my life and the life of those closest to me, is something I now more fully recognise. Many of my reactions have been an adjustment to that. Any trauma is powerful and can have long-lasting repercussions, and as soon as I recognised – and accepted – that there were strong elements of trauma involved, it has helped me to move on.

As I have described in an earlier chapter, I had realised that the diagnosis and all that came after triggered a real sense of grief. To my earlier list, I could add purpose, friendship groups and support network. A lot of my friendships had previously come through my teamwork in Church ministry, simply by virtue of the fact that we met and prayed regularly about whatever we were involved in at the time. I guess some people in similar situations to mine, could lose for example the camaraderie they had at the gym, or running club, going to pubs or clubs, eating out regularly together, or similar activities- social friendships, I suppose, I might call them. Some friendships will survive and deepen, some will fade. No unkindness here, simply less in common now, or 'busyness' for the healthy ones precludes time for much else. Conversely, it is possible to find new friendships. I am fortunate to have some very good friends who have stuck with me and simply changed the meeting opportunities, but many are not so fortunate. But I do think, on reflection, that a person's support network can also change because of long-term health issues.

The term "back to normal" is not always useful as I have

discovered. For years I tried to get back to normal, 'as it was'. But can any of us *ever* do that? Every experience of our lives affects us, changes and develops us, takes us in one direction or another. We are living creatures, who can in a sense, never remain exactly the same person as we were yesterday because we are constantly growing. Consider this: a child has a toy roughly snatched from them for the first time, whilst playing with a friend. It's a pretty normal learning experience. Prior to this, it probably never crossed their mind that such a thing could happen. There may be tears or a tantrum. Or withdrawal and fear. Such a child learns that everyone is not always kind, and that they are not the centre of everyone's universe (as they seem to think when they are babies!!)

What was the response of the adults around at the time?

Or other children?

Many factors will determine the reaction.

And it is logged away as a memory.

Will they become more timid in future?

Or fearful?

Do they start choosing to play alone, or get defensive with their toys?

Do they fight back?

Do they become a snatcher themselves to survive?

The innocent child they were before, in one sense, has gone.

That memory is there.

They now know something more about the world they live in than they did before and thus they adapt.

As I think about this picture, I see a tiny microcosm of the Garden of Eden as described in Genesis the first book of the Bible. Innocence removed and consequences follow. Things once seen cannot be unseen, or things experienced cannot be erased.

As soon as I realised that getting back to normal was not my aim, I started thinking in terms of aspiring to reach my potential. It might well look different from what it would have pre-2014 but I could still have the "life in all its fullness" that Jesus offers. (John 10:10, GNT). I remember distinctly some words from my hospital counsellor. I had been describing the uncertainty I felt about what was going on. Was I getting better? Was I not? How my parameters seemed to change on a regular basis, not knowing from day to day how I would feel. My inability, as I saw it, to plan anything. Her words were, 'It seems to me you've only got one option' and that was, 'Embrace the chaos that is your life'!

Embrace the chaos? That was about as alien to my ordered character as I could imagine. But we talked it through and it began to make some sense and seemed to be quite simple really. A fundamental shift for me certainly, as it involved letting go of so many expectations that I had for any particular day. Letting go of others' expectations of me (real or assumed). Accepting not fighting. Being real. There *will* be bad days. Be real. And what, for goodness sake is 'normal' anyway?

The other counsellor that I spoke to concurrently was a wonderful Christian lady with whom I could talk openly about my worries regarding my perceived lack of faith, doubts and fears. She described what I had been going through, and was beginning to come out of, as being like going through a wilderness. I had never thought of it like that, but when we read the Exodus story of the Israelites travelling through wilderness to the Promised Land[12], they didn't know how to get where they were going. We see that they were totally dependent on God throughout. They were guided by a pillar of cloud in the day, and a pillar of fire by night. They were fed supernaturally with the manna and quails. Water came from a rock when they had none. Obstacles such as the Red Sea were removed to enable progress in the journey. It was different simply *because* they were in the wilderness. Like them, I was not supposed to know. I was supposed to lean on God and follow His direction. And that I was doing.

When moving into the realm of "What if" or "If only", she reminded me of a verse from Philippians, which reads:

"Being confident of this, (*i.e. your partnership in the gospel from the first day until now*) He who began a good work in you will carry it on to completion until the day of Christ Jesus."

---

[12] The story of the Israelites journey through the wilderness can be found in the Bible in the book of Exodus.

Philippians 1:6 (NIV)
(*information in italics added by me*)

When the Israelites arrived in the Promised Land, they worked the land for their food, they searched for water and they couldn't expect God to remove every obstacle in their way. If they came to a sea, they would need to cross it in a more conventional way! God would still be guiding, but differently. I began to feel as if I were coming out of that wilderness place; things seemed lighter. More do-able. How we need others and their talents at different times in our lives. And I must conclude that others need mine too. I still have a purpose.

Whilst in hospital very ill, God had been exceptionally close. I had needed that at the time. But now, I was in my 'new land' and having to seek God's guidance in another way. Sometimes He carries us, and I'm so thankful that He does. Sometimes He guides. Sometimes He will save us from our mistakes, or a problem ahead; other times He allows us to make the mistake in order that we may learn from it. He wants us all, whatever our circumstances, to grow. And growing means adapting and changing. And don't we so often learn and grow the most during the tougher times?

My latest conversations with the doctors toward the end of 2023, centred around 3 topics.

1) The fact that chemo (or possibly tablet) side effects seem to be having an accumulative negative effect. I was beginning to dread those weeks of treatment.

2) This led to the question: If this is still an acute form of leukaemia, and hence could have an end point, what are we waiting for? When will you know to take me off the chemo? It was explained to me that they were trying to minimise the chances of the leukaemia returning by keeping me on the treatment. As always, it was very difficult, maybe impossible, to actually get to a point when they can say it is totally safe to withdraw from the chemo. Basically, the more I have, the more chance that the disease can be kept at bay.

3) Finally, being acutely aware that the chemo itself is toxic, and thus harming good cells in my body as well as the diseased ones, I surmised that surely there has

to be an end point. With regard to this there was a definitive answer: I would not be on this chemotherapy longer than two years. Did I think I could keep going until June?

I have always appreciated their honesty. If they don't know, they don't know. That is the current arrangement. Unless the effects get too bad for me to cope with treatment, I am on this 5-week regime until June 2024. What will happen after then? After those 2 years? We don't know. It reminds me of some lyrics in the old Johnny Nash song, "There are more questions than answers".

So now, if I am asked, how can I live with the uncertainty, the answer varies.

Sometimes, I can't, and the whole situation becomes overwhelming.

Sometimes I think totally logically, in that none of us can know what lies ahead, so I'm no different, except that my previous assumptions that I would enjoy a long and active life had been rather shattered.

Mostly, I cope by taking each day as it comes, taking everything to God in prayer, and intentionally being thankful as I go about my daily life.

Whilst pottering in the garden, I would remember a time when I longed to even get outdoors, let alone lift a hoe.

Sitting on a bus, I will be remembering a time I wondered if I would ever do such mundane things again.

Being stuck in a traffic queue, I find myself being thankful that I can be independent enough to drive.

Although I cannot claim that I am able to do this 100% of the time, I can honestly say, I see blessings in so many more tiny things in life, in a way I did not before I became ill.

This is coming to the end of my story of the journey with leukaemia so far. At school I was taught that every story has a beginning, middle and an end. So, I am going to finish now in the time-honoured tradition, with what I think is an appropriate adjustment.

THE END...

... OR IS IT?

I remember being taught once years ago, in a sermon I think, that there are so many things in the Bible we don't understand, so many things about God and life that we will never know. And we can be tempted to keep looking for answers where there are none, so busy arguing, debating and getting nowhere, that we miss working with what we DO know. We have plenty we can be working with!

So, what **do** I know?

God is good.

He knows me. He knows all my struggles.

God is ultimately in control of the world and its destiny.

He is infinitely more powerful than leukaemia.

God loves me.

I know this because of what Jesus did for me at the cross.

I may not understand everything that is happening to me – or in the world as a whole- but God is faithful.

God knows how this story will proceed.

He has never let me down yet. I can do what I can do, and trust Him with the rest.

I remind myself of some words from The Bible:

John 3:16

Romans 8:35-37

Philipians 4:4-7

And I know that I have an eternal home with Him when this life is over.

And that is my future.

"Then I saw 'a new heaven and a new earth', for the first heaven and the first earth had passed away, and there was no longer any sea. I saw the Holy City, the new Jerusalem, coming down out of heaven from God, prepared as a bride beautifully dressed for her husband. And I heard a loud voice from the throne saying, "Look! God's dwelling place is now among the people, and he will dwell with them. They will be his people, and God himself will be with them and be their

God. He will wipe every tear from their eyes. There will be no more death or mourning or crying or pain, for the old order of things has passed away."

He who was seated on the throne said, 'I am making everything new!' Then he said, 'Write this down, for these words are trustworthy and true'. He said to me: 'It is done. I am the Alpha and the Omega, the Beginning and the End. To the thirsty I will give water without cost from the spring of the water of life. Those who are victorious will inherit all this, and I will be their God and they will be my children' ."

Revelation 21:1-7 (NIV)

And to that there is NO END

Derek:

Where was God in all this? I have never really thought too deeply about this because from the start I knew where He was, right in the middle of it, with us. How do I know? Why do I think this? Am I trying to be super spiritual? Have I got super faith?

I will try to answer but in reverse order. Have I got super faith? No, I have mustard seed faith, but God is faithful.

Am I being super spiritual? I don't think so, we were in a practical situation with practical help from a God who is alive and loves us.

Why do I think He was right in the middle of this? Because there was rarely a time, if ever, that I was afraid. Even when Jane had a tetany attack (involuntary muscle contractions) before the proposed transplant, passing out, her eyes rolling, her hands going weird and her body shaking, and surrounded by the crash team, the Sister said she was calm, because I was calm, when I told her what the problem was and how to deal with it. That was God. The same was true when Jane had another attack in the shower when we were at home and she broke her toe. I was calm, called the hospital and got Jane on the bed, ready for when the ambulance arrived. The calmness wasn't from me, it was God with me, Immanuel.

How do I know? Too many things have been way beyond my natural strength and ability. The timing of events, even bad things, especially bad things have been perfect. My deep depression was before all this started. My retirement from teaching was before all this started. The passing of our much-loved Nanny Kath was before this started. The start of my part time job in admin was just as the whole experience began, but I could work away from the office. Jen learned to drive and passed her test very quickly (incredible) and bought a new car in no time at all and was also allowed to work away from the office. I know God was in this from the start because I more than managed, when I should have, could have sunk, I sailed through so much. Jen said I looked shattered etc. but I never felt that way. God held me up through it all, like Moses' arms!

I learned how much I loved Jane through this. I hadn't known before. And I learned how much God loves us too. I hadn't understood that before either.

Jenny:

When Mum and I spoke, I never heard her say she was scared of dying. But she was scared of leaving us all behind and how we would all cope and she was worried about being sick all the time. She would say she felt frustrated when people said she was being brave and being an inspiration, and I would nod understandingly, but truth be told – she was (and still is) an inspiration, and I think she handled it all brilliantly. (She'll probably edit that out!).

George:

Ten years on from those earlier conversations, Esther and I still call Leicester home. We've both finished our degrees, lived in six different houses (four rented and two with a family), welcomed our amazing son, Benjamin, and experienced so much life that was never really "part of the plan." When I reflect on Mum's journey with leukaemia, I experience a wide range of emotions. I'm filled with sadness for the many moments she missed due to this terrible disease. There were times when I feared losing her, and I felt anger at the injustice of the situation. Why did this have to happen?

However, I'm also awestruck by my Mum and Dad's strength and resilience over the journey. It's incredible how many times we've been blessed with more time together. We've shared laughter and jokes as a family, and every day, week, month, and year has felt like an enormous blessing. Mum has had the joy of holding our baby boy, and for a while in 2014, that seemed impossible. Mum's diagnosis in 2014 has meant that our lives took a far different path than we could've imagined. My predominant emotion is one of gratitude, that Mum was gifted with more time, and we could share it with her.

Esther:

God has been gracious to me. He's challenged many of the things I believed about myself and helped me to look beyond the things I could see. I am still a planner. I still like to know what to expect. But I have also learnt to be flexible and to trust God with his plans. There are still things about all of this that I don't understand. Things I feel sad about… things I regret. But I hold on to God, knowing his understanding is beyond anything I can comprehend and trusting that his plans for me are good because he loves me and my family.

An:

Oh where to start and what to say about Jane, how she inspires me and how precious she is in my life? There is just so much about this wonderful lady that it's really difficult to know where to begin. I suppose that a good place would be to start by thanking God for our friendship. So here goes:

Thank You, Father, that when we least expect it you put people alongside each other to share part of a journey. I thank You constantly that You engineered mine and Jane's paths (or trenches) to come alongside each other and to remain parallel for the distance that only You know the length of. Thank You Father that as we share a friendship and walk alongside each other You are with us every step of the way. Amen.

When Jane first received the news that she had leukaemia and was going through the early rounds of treatment we weren't actually friends. Oh, we knew each other through church and I was as shocked as anybody by the news, I was also glad that I was able to help in some small way by providing a photo book of landscapes (when asked by her daughter Jenny) for her to browse through and paint if she chose too. I thank You too Father for those wonderful people that she had alongside her during that time.

To be honest I can't remember what year it was that our friendship started but I do know that it was after a trip to a New Wine summer conference that Jane asked if I'd be her prayer buddy. I'm so glad that she asked and that I said yes, the rest as they say is history. From our meeting once a week for about an hour to pray together it now seems impossible to spend less than at least a couple of hours together (more than once a week) enjoying coffee, chatting, praying and reading the Bible together.

Thank You so much Father that You put Jane in my life and that You are the one that holds, comforts and gives strength to her and her family and that you are the rock they stand on. Thank You that with all that she has gone through and is going through that her light shines brightly and reflects Your glory and love onto those around her, that includes me and I am so grateful for it. Now that I've got started I could ramble on for ages but as I'm only meant to be writing a brief piece I'd better stop now.

Sue Angell:

At the time of Jane's diagnosis I viewed her as one of my spiritual guides as I was a member of her house group, as well as a friend. With a nursing background, I was frightened by the sudden diagnosis of leukaemia. I understood the threat. Also as a carer (awful word) for my husband, I felt concern for Jane's husband. In some ways I felt I understood more of his concerns, although my mother had been diagnosed, years ago, with leukaemia and had survived for many years. Following many months of hospital treatment and many prayers, I realised how much I missed seeing her, and selfishly, how much I missed her wisdom!

A stem cell transplant appeared to be a miracle from God. When its good effects stopped working, I was not surprised, but I felt 'gutted' for Jane, her husband and family whom I had begun to know. The second transplant was a miracle. The German male donor was included in our prayers.

Jane has been back leading our group for some time. Now I just feel a huge love for her. Interestingly, I also feel a great empathy for her husband. I know the deep, deep worry of walking beside the person you love most, watching their endless trials, wanting to take them away, yet knowing that is never possible. Their journey confirms to me again that the greatest trials test us, faith sustains us and love conquers.

Jane P:

We did go out for coffee again – though not for some time. It was a significant day for us both, I think, and Jane was excited to go out. It was a promise we had made to each other in those early days when the future was so uncertain – I don't know about her, but for me, it was something to hold onto: we would go out for coffee again, a symbol of moving forward together. Looking ahead:

I am so grateful for Jane in my life. We have been through some hugely challenging times together and I don't pretend that this is over for her. I am grateful for the extra years we have had, for coffee and lunch trips, for long phone calls, for visits in the garden after Covid and for being able to share hugs again. I am grateful to God for bringing her this far – for not leaving us when times were tough, for holding us when hope was fragile, for giving us new memories to celebrate together.

Rob:

It is strange to look back on Mum being ill with leukaemia over the last few years, because it was all so tangled up in normal life. People were getting married, children being born, even a lockdown more recently. Our family living a couple of hours away meant that I didn't face it in the same way as, say, Dad, or members of their Church. Instead, it hit home in those gaps when life stopped. Then it was like hearing the news again each time. The rest of the time it was in the background and I suppose it made me feel tired. In the same way you feel tired overdoing a book or jigsaw, rather than all cried out. I thought about it more than I felt about it. Going home or seeing Mum in a hospital bed was a starker reminder each time, and then it was strange to see how normal it seemed for Mum and Dad; normal for a leukaemia household, at least. Of course, I was sometimes sad, especially when others around me were.

When Mum was first diagnosed, me, Jen and George all went home and prayed, with Dad there too, and our church in St Ives prayed. And after that I didn't really worry about it anymore. Genuinely. Not that I am a very brave person who doesn't let things get to him! Ask Elspeth. But if we're talking "big things", breakdown in relationships, marriages, in churches and amongst friends and family members upset me much, much more. My own faults bother me. Mum and I will live forever and I have settled that in my mind long before she was ill, and even more firmly since. It is now to me as if she always exists. I believe Jesus Christ's own words on this subject. It is sin that separates us from God and each other, not death as such. If I can compare it to anything, it is like knowing your loved ones are already safe in a dire emergency. It is a mixture of grief, hope, adrenalin, yes — but also a sense of relief, gratitude and peace.

I am also grateful for so many things at a practical level. For the bone marrow donor. For my parents' marriage. For Dave and Jane's help, and all those at their Church also. For the fact all this happened when Jen, George and I were adults, and not children; and my parents older parents, not younger ones—something I am truly grateful for. Not everyone has that.

All this remains true today. I always pray that Mum will recover fully from this leukaemia, so that she feels well, that she and Dad enjoy a freer lifestyle, and to round off the story God started. God is wiser, and He may choose to do otherwise. Absolutely my main prayer is that Mum and my whole family would know how much God loves them, that He forgives every sin, can reverse every problem, and how throughout every moment that has gone by, whilst some of us have weakened and aged, and others literally grown up, He is not changed in the least.

Pat:

You are my treasured friend and I will stay on this rollercoaster ride with you always.

EPILOGUE

I have spoken of doctors and nurses, Churches and prayers, family and friends and God himself. But there is someone else in this story.

My donor.

In 2014, I was told just 4 things about my donor.

1) He is a man
2) He is from Germany
3) He was at the time 54 years old
4) His cells were a nigh-on perfect match to mine

But I also know from his actions that he has been kind-hearted; enough to offer some of his cells to a stranger in England- twice. There are still frozen cells waiting in a hospital freezer should I ever have need of them.

I did write a letter to him after each transplant and sent the letter to the Anthony Nolan charity through which my match was found. I wanted to and needed to express my thanks, and I can only hope he received the letters.

So, I don't know much about him at all. But God knows him. And I pray that God will bless him greatly for what he offered to me – the chance of further life. Because without donors like him, more people like me would die, too soon.

POSTSCRIPT: MAY 2024

So, what does my life look like today?
The doctors and I have agreed to stop the chemotherapy as the negative effects were indeed beginning to outweigh the positive.

I am currently in remission. What an amazing privilege that is, after nearly ten years!

In practical terms, my life is rebuilt; in as much as I have learned how to live better within the limits of what I can and cannot do.

Learning German has continued as a hobby and as an intellectual challenge, to say the very least!

Derek has created a paved area where my vegetable patch used to be. Let's get real here - I am unlikely to be starting up any heavy digging at my age anyway! I am learning to 'potter' in the garden. Befitting my recent status as a pensioner! A few veg can be grown in pots, I am told. (Who knew??) There's always something new to learn when one door closes.

I have always found playing the piano to be a great way to relax and unwind; I do more of that. And I certainly don't miss the technical practice that was required when teaching pupils of Grade 8 standard and upwards! I simply enjoy the experience.

Over the years I have enjoyed doing cross-stitch. Even prior to my diagnosis, my eyesight was proving a challenge. Since 2014, I have consciously moved over to doing more wool tapestry work, helped along by being given two gifts of tapestry kits during my recovery period.

Art Club is back on my calendar. Two hours a week of friendship and painting. I miss more meetings than I would like but remain very thankful for their gracious acceptance of my situation.

At home I love to paint; although (and I still don't fully understand it of myself), I always seem to be more conscious of what "ought to be done" and allow those tasks to take priority.

Every morning, however, is new, and provides me with a chance to reset my thinking with the ongoing help of God and others. I have produced some of my paintings as cards which I sell where I can to raise a little money for the Church and the two hospitals responsible for my care. I have even been fortunate enough to sell some paintings for this same purpose; none of this amounts to much financially but is my small way of saying thank you.

Meeting with An and praying together has become a regular part of my staple diet of life.

I have been able to continue with the Life Group I have spoken about. They continue to be a significant part of my support, and I hope I can be of some encouragement to them in return.

There has, for many reasons, been a demise in letter-writing. But a hand-written letter or card dropping on to someone's mat can be a great joy for an elderly (or ill) person who gets out little. As I was encouraged and lifted by postcards from Rosie and others as they go on holidays, etc, I find myself in a position to do a similar favour to others.

I make more of a conscious effort to keep in phone contact with people when I can. I see friends less often than I would like for practical reasons – but I can still talk to them on the mobile. (I could do this even during the times I was in bed, as long as I didn't inadvertently press the wrong icon and make a video call - my technology skills have sadly not made a significant amount of progress!) I have been surprised on many occasions, by opportunities to pray with people on the phone. I have also found that older people will talk very freely about worries over illness, age and dying, not despite my situation, but perhaps specifically because of it.

I have written a book. My hope being, that by sharing my experience, it might serve as a comfort or help to others in some small way. I am reminded of some words of the apostle Paul in Corinthians, which reads:

"Praise be to the God and Father of our Lord Jesus Christ, the Father of compassion and the God of all comfort, who comforts us in all our troubles, so that we can comfort those in any trouble with the comfort we ourselves receive from God."

2 Corinthians 1:3-4 (NIV)

From the beginning of all this, so many years ago, all I could see was a gaping hole in my life from how I had filled my hours. A gap where my ministry at Young at Heart had been. And although I held a belief that God had a purpose for me, it was unknown to me back then.

Many activities needed to be stopped.

Some have been picked up again.

Some have simply changed in method.

New things have grown.

Yes, my life looks different now. And it is a full life. God has found me a new way.

My Faith

My faith in God has been challenged and honed. To say I have learned a lot during this period seems an understatement. It is as if my previously held beliefs have been strengthened from within and underneath. Underpinned.

Recently, our Church had two TV screens installed, prior to which the fittings needed to be strength - tested. The testing involved hanging weights from said fittings, which were way beyond what would be required by a screen. If they could hold the weight of approximately 35kg for 24 hours, the weight of a mere screen would pose no problem.

Whatever holds us up in our lives, it seems, also needs to be able to handle whatever weighty challenge we may be faced with. At this particular moment in time, it feels to me as if I have been through a ten-year process of strength-testing. If God can bring me through what I have already experienced, it gives me some confidence that whatever lies ahead - and there will inevitably be future struggles and pressures – God can take the weight of it. If I trust Him enough to let Him.

Take this morning for an example. It is May 2024. I presently have a chest infection for which I am on yet another course of antibiotics.

My friend Pat quipped,

'You'll look like an antibiotic soon!'

To which my response was,

'Between you and me, there's a race going on in my body… Which will I get to resemble first? An antibiotic? Or a colander?'

You must laugh sometimes!

Following a particularly deep cough three days ago, I noticed a pea-sized lump in my abdomen, around which there was evidence of a minor bleed under the skin. Whilst having this checked out today, it was discovered that there was a harder 'something' underneath.

It is probably totally innocuous.

It might not be.

I await an MRI scan to determine what it is.

Would it be strange to find I was concerned about finding a new, if tiny, lump? Yet God's word tells us we have no need to remain anxious or worried. Yesterday in preparation for my trip to the hospital today, a passage of scripture came to mind.

[4] "Rejoice in the Lord always. I will say it again: rejoice!

[5] Let your gentleness be evident to all.

The Lord is near.

[6] Do not be anxious about anything, but in every situation, by prayer and petition, with thanksgiving, present your requests to God.

[7] And the peace of God, which transcends all understanding, will guard your hearts and your minds in Christ Jesus"

Philippians 4:4-7 (NIV)

I decided - and it was a decision, an act of the will – to trust it. Just do it. What did I have to lose?

I started to praise and thank God for who He is, and for all He had already done for me.

For what He daily does for us all, through the wonderful world of nature.

As always, for my husband Derek, family, and friends on whom I can call to pray.

For all at the Sandra Chapman Centre, always working on our behalf. Today I was added to their already busy list. I told Him I wished it hadn't had to be so, as I hated being that 'extra' patient with something basically exploratory. But I thanked God for them and prayed for His blessing on them all.

I thanked God for so many things which will never change, such as His love for us, including me.

I was encouraged by the four words hidden in those few verses to the Philippians, "The Lord is near".

Within this framework, I brought to God my prayer and petition.

I wanted to be OK.

I wanted to go home.

I was scared to think of further potential trouble ahead.

I told Him everything I could think of.

And I waited to see if the promise of verse 7 would be the result. I had done my bit. Now it was up to Him.

As I prayed during this time at the hospital, I was reminded of something I'd heard. I couldn't remember whether it was just a feel-good saying, or something actually from the Bible. So while at the hospital, I rang a friend and asked her to find out for me, and text through the result. Some 10-15 minutes later I read the following text about which I had enquired:

"These are the words of him who is holy and true, who holds the key of David. What he opens no one can shut, and what he shuts no one can open"

Revelation 3:7 (NIV)

During the hours at the hospital I reminded myself of these words.

Basically God knows.

My past.

My present.

And most importantly for me at this moment, my future.

If the door to a healthier life ahead is opened by God, no-one can shut it.

If He shuts that door, no amount of pushing or shoving from me will make a scrap of difference.

Nor will any of my worrying. It would simply be a waste of my precious energy.

And guess what?

The promise of verse seven became a reality for me at that very moment.

[6] Do not be anxious about anything, but in every situation, by prayer and petition, with thanksgiving, present your requests to God.

[7] And the peace of God, which transcends all understanding, will guard your hearts and your minds in Christ Jesus"

Philippians 4:6-7 (NIV)

Final Words

Without any warning, life can indeed take a completely different turn. An unseen illness causing a tsunami - like effect.

I am constantly learning how to walk faithfully and honestly with God - and others - through a long-term 'invisible' illness

Because what you see is not always how it is.

My world is different now. And so am I.

And from wondering if I would ever meet our second grandchild, I have recently met grandchild number five!

And Derek and I thank God for it all.

**As of September 2024,
I am still battling with the Leukaemia.**

The 'Mill Family', August 2023

The Five Grandchildren, April 2024

WHO'S WHO IN THIS STORY?

Derek: is my husband. We have been married for almost 46 years, and in the latter ten of these particularly, he has been my rock. "We're in this together"

Rob/Robert: is our eldest son. A constant support for me (and many others I imagine) and often a giver of wise and godly counsel.

Elspeth: is married to Rob. It has been said, 'Behind every great man is a great woman'. I think there may be some truth in this, Elspeth. Thank you.

Jen/Jenny: is our one and only daughter. I couldn't wish for one better or kinder. A gem. She has been a sounding board for me on many an occasion, especially throughout the process of writing this book.

Sam: is Jen's husband. A good and honest man. Together they make a very special couple.

George: is our youngest son. A talented and kind young man, who has had to face many challenges through his life, I am a proud mum. (And he has patience with me beyond belief when it comes to technology!)

Esther: is George's wife. This 10-year story has been the backdrop of their marriage from its very beginning. To say this has not been easy for them is an understatement. She is remarkable.

Jane P: moved to Belton with her young family about 30 years ago, and has been a firm friend ever since.

Rosie: is the rector of our Church. From the very outset she quickly put into action focussed prayer in the Church. For this I am very grateful.

Pat:	has been a faithful friend for some 40 years. Her message to me? "Friends walk together"
An:	is a more recent friendship. An and I meet twice a week to chat and pray together. Our friendship has grown throughout my illness, and has been invaluable.
Shirley:	I met Shirley at Young at Heart, only to find she has lived but a few doors away from me for the last 22 years! She is a member of the Life Group I belong to, and I am privileged to have her as a friend.
Sue A:	is also a member of the Church and the Life Group I am in. She has given me some very sage advice over these years. A very wise lady.
Sue B:	is another Christian lady who has been a good friend to me. She is a real prayer warrior and has prayed for me (along with many, many others) throughout the whole decade. Thank you.

Printed in Great Britain
by Amazon